Nap

400 Wi

The Maps

Chapters

Napa Valley Winery Maps
400 Winery Directory,
Touring & Tasting Tips
Ralph & Lahni DeAmicis
Authors of the Dream Tour Series

Published by
Cuore Libre Publishing
Napa, California

To Order Copies visit
www.AmicisTours.com

Disclaimer: We create these books through extensive research that includes having visited many of these wineries multiple times. But we make no guarantees for the accuracy of the information included herein, and accept no responsibility for any losses or inconvenience you may suffer from using this product. Important: Our advice is intended to help you stay safe while you enjoy the region, but mixing alcohol and driving is a risky endeavor. We suggest that you approach it cautiously by having a designated or professional driver. We want you to have a fun time in Wine Country and come back and visit again and again.

Ralph & Lahni DeAmicis

The Napa Valley Map Key

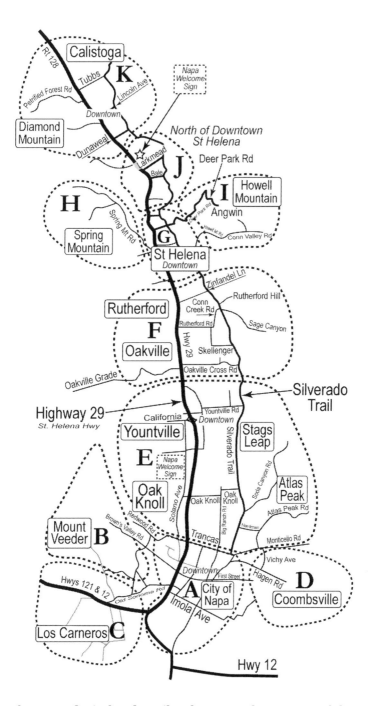

The Dotted Circles describe the general coverage of the maps but they often overlap. Some zones have multiple maps that split the areas into east and west, with detailed maps of the nearest downtowns. These are not based on the borders of the American Viticulture Areas but are arranged for ease of navigation.

The Southern Napa Valley
Crossroads & American Viticulture Areas

The Napa Downtown, with its navigable river, and the oldest residential areas stretch generally from Imola Avenue north to Trancas Street, and from Jefferson Street east to the Silverado Trail. To the west are the hills of Mount Veeder (Map C) and Los Carneros (Map B), and to the east are the rolling hills of Coombsville (Map D).

Note 1: On the maps the names of the AVA's (American Viticulture Areas) are enclosed in solid, framed boxes. Some AVA's are the names of towns, but some are not.
Note 2: The maps are not always to scale.

The Northern Napa Valley
Crossroads & American Viticulture Areas

The crossroads are essential for navigating the valley. On heavy traffic weekends, when everyone has been drinking, they allow you to always make safer right-hand turns. Generally, the main crossroads are about a mile apart.

The Miracle of Downtown Napa

For years, tourists on the way to the valley simply drove past downtown Napa. It hadn't been developed as a destination because of the many devasting floods it had endured since its founding in 1847. Smart shopkeepers kept sandbags handy. In 2005 the city enlisted the help of the Army Core of Engineers, while pitching its tourist potential to the big hotel chains. Today, flood free Napa sports great hotels, shopping, restaurants, theaters and some say the greatest density of winery tasting rooms on the planet. It is an exciting place to visit and taste wine!

Getting Around the Downtown

Main Street parallels the Napa River while First Street crosses it on the bridge connecting the old downtown in the west with the newer Oxbow District to the east that was developed after the river was tamed. Downtown Napa has abundant parking, shown on the map, surrounding the center. There are four main tourist areas, and each has its own personality and unique attractions. On the following pages we describe them and list some of the tasting rooms and restaurants you will find there.

1) **First Street between Coombs and School Streets** is where you will find the most expensive tasting rooms and shopping. The **Andaz** and **Archer** are both large premium hotels with their own restaurants. A large shopping area, with the visitor center, wraps around the Archer between Coombs Street and Franklin Street. The Uptown 'Concert' Theater is on 3rd Street.

Restaurants: Tarla (Mediterranean Bar & Grill), Oenotri (Northern Italian), Norman Rose (Sports), Grace's Table (great breakfast), Compline (Wine Centric), Sky & Vine Rooftop Bar (Archer), Eiko (Japanese), Kitchen Door, Kenzo (Japanese), Anette's Chocolate, Petit Soleil (Breakfast & Lunch).

Tasting Rooms: Jam Cellars, John Anthony, Outland (Group), Outer Space Wine Shop, Gentleman Farmer, Roots Run Deep, Robert Craig, Padis, Cadet, Wine Girls, Kerr (Pro Golfer), Ellman, Levendi, Vineyard 29, California Brandy House, Mayacamas, Acumen, Alpha Omega, Rebel Vintners (Group), Shadowbox, Fess Parker, Mia Carta (Group), Brown Family. On Second Street between School & Franklin are these very cool tasting rooms, Bubbles, Benevolent Neglect, Fayard, Gamling & McDuck. Jeffries General Store.

2) **Main Street from First Street to Caymus Street** is home to the **Blue Note Jazz Club** at the south end and at the north end the **Vintner's Collective**. This includes First Street from the bridge west to Caymus Street.

Restaurants: Napa Valley Bistro, The Q Restaurant & Bar, Azzurro Pizzeria, Hal Yamashita (Japanese), Croccante Pizza, Cole's Chop House (Steakhouse), Torc (American), Taqueria Rosita, Osha Thai, Napa Palisades Saloon, Bounty Hunter Wine Bar & BBQ, Wilfred's Lounge (Island Cuisine), Don Perico (Mexican), Allegria (Italian), Napa Noodles, Scala (Italian), Small World (Middle Eastern) Jax Diner, Barnhouse Napa Brews (coffee & wine), Starbucks.

Tasting Rooms: Vintner's Collective is Napa's first group tasting room with an excellent selection of small wineries. Housley Family, Azur, Saint Clair, Boutique du Vin, New Frontier, Bazan Cellars, T Vine, Back Room Wines shop, Vermeil Wines (football Coach), Chateau Buena Vista of Sonoma, Napa Valley Distillery (Cocktails).

3) **Main Street from 2nd Street, south to the end.** This area **borders the river** and there is a lovely walkway that runs the length of it from First Street to the point where the **Napa River Inn** sits. Veteran's Park was created as part of the river remediation to prevent flooding. If the water runs too high, it can overflow and be contained in the amphitheater of the park. From 2nd to 3rd, opposite Veteran's Park is **restaurant row**. From 3rd to 5th is a wonderful mix of even more eateries and shopping.

Restaurants: From 2nd to 3rd are Downtown Joes Pub, Carpe Diem (New American), Le Paris Cafe (Bakery) Napkins Bar & Grill, Zu Zu (Tapas), Hank's Take Away, La Taberna (Spanish) and Velo Pizzeria. From 3rd to 5th are Morimoto Asia, Napa Roastery Cafe, Waterfront Seafood Grill, Entrecot (Argentinian), Los Agaves (Mexican), Morimoto (Japanese Iron Chef). The **Napa River Hotel** building includes four restaurants, Celadon (Eclectic), Angele (French), the General Store (Breakfast & Lunch) and Sweetie Pie's Bakery.

Tasting Rooms: Quilt and Company at 3rd and Main. Ackerman on Randolph Street.

4) **East First Street:** This is the eastern end of 1st Street over the bridge from the downtown. The **Oxbow Market** is filled with artisan markets and places to get something good to eat to take away or enjoy at the tables inside. There are also gift and books shops and it's a busy place. At the **Culinary Institute of America** downtown campus there are a wide variety of food and wine programs for the community including places to eat and taste wine.

Restaurants: Gott's Burgers, Model Bakery, Fillipi's Pizza Grotto, Hog Island Oyster, Eiko's (Sushi), C Casa (Mexican), Bar Lucia (Small Bites), El Porteno (Latin American) Kara's Cupcakes, Live Fire Pizza, Loveski's Deli, Oxbow Cheese, Olive Press, Ritual Roasters (Coffee), Anette's Chocolates.

Tasting Rooms: The Wine Thief, (Group) Walt Wines, Trade Brewing, Fieldwork Brewing, Gustavo Wine, Krupp Brothers, Mark Herold, Feast it Forward (Group).

About the CIA: Copia was originally *The American Center for Wine, Food & the Arts* from 2001 to 2008. It became part of the CIA in 2015. Copia, Roman Goddess of wealth and abundance.

Mount Veeder is a heavily wooded, mountainous region reached on small winding roads. It's unique among Napa's Bordeaux style grape growing areas due to its basaltic geology. That alkaline influence lets it produce softer and less tannic Cabernets than many in Napa, mostly grown predominantly on volcanic soils. The mountain was formed when plates of ancient seabed were crushed together and pushed up into ridges. Mount Veeder is the first mountain complex north of the bay. Its highest ridge extends quite far north and you can see it when you look west from Yountville.

The next mountain north (to your right) is St. John, an ancient volcano and a contemporary of St. Helena, that lords over the northern part of the Valley. Hess Persson Estate, with its extensive modern art museum, is the only large winery on Mount Veeder and if you are an art lover it's worth the trip. The region includes number excellent family wineries and the world class Mayacamas Vineyards.

Los Carneros, or 'The Rams', first appeared on a map in an 1820's Spanish land grant. Apparently, they felt this would be a good place for grazing sheep. It was considered too cold and windy for growing grapes. Then, in the 1970's growers began planting cool loving vines like Chardonnay and Pinot Noir with good results. The soil sits on an ancient basalt seabed and the area is subject to strong winds off the bay. The results are grapes with excellent acid and bright flavors. This is the only American Viticulture Area shared by Napa and Sonoma.

Coombsville is Napa's newest AVA and among the most convenient from the downtown, starting just outside the city limits on the east side of town. The region sits inside an ancient volcanic caldera and, like Los Carneros, it was once considered too cool for grapes, and instead was used for grazing horses and other livestock. Today the Bordeaux style grapes are widely planted on small family vineyards and wineries.

See E2 for
the west side

See E3 for
the east side

Rector Resevoir

Vine Cliff

Dwyer Rd
Paradigm
Yount Mill Rd
Napa Cellars
Cosentino
Mustards (R)
Kellerer
Brix (R)

Piazza
DelDotto

Yountville

Paraduxx

Washington St
Goosecross

State Lane

Gemstone

Tom
Scott

Poetry
Inn (H)

Dominus
Madison St (H)

Yountville Cross Rd

Robert
Sinskey?
Sold 2023

Blankiet

Cliff Lede

Downtown
Yountville

Yount Street

Baldacci

(H)

Market

(H)

Domaine
Chandon

Shafer

(H)
(H)

Silverado

Quioxte

Veterans
Home of
California

California Dr
Vintner's
Golf Course

Vineyard View Dr
Keever

Taylor

Odette

Robinson

Stags
Leap
Winery

Washington Street

Pine
Ridge

Bell

Realm

Stags Leap

Hill Family
Elyse

Hoffman Ln

Mira

Stag's Leap
Cellars

Regusci

Antica

Hoffman Ln
The Setting Inn (H)

Chimney Rock

Darms
Lane

The Cottages
At Napa Valley (H)
Darms Ln

Silverado Trail

Clos
Du Val

The Caves
at
Soda Canyon

Hunter
Glenn

Silenus

Oak Knoll

Relic

Arrow &
Branch

White Rock

Trefethen

Oak Knoll Rd

James Cole
Signorello

Loma Vista

Laird

Oak Knoll Rd

Matetra

Darioush

O'Brien

Monticello

Hagafen

Soda Canyon Rd

Orchard Ave

Hwy 29

Lewis

Black
Stallion

Market

Solano Ave

Ashes &
Diamonds

Fortunati

Back
Stage

Robert
Biale

Seven
Apart

Ellman

William
Hill

Salvador Road

Boyd

Reynolds

Atlas Peak Rd

Krupp

Silverado
Resort

Big Ranch Rd

Burgess

Hardman Rd

Market

Redwood

Market
Whole Foods

Bread &
Butter

Cefani

Razi

Wetstone
Del Dotto Caves

Trancas Rd

Eleven
Eleven

Judd's
Hill

Jarvis   3 miles

Napa

Soscal Ave

Hyde de
Villaine

Beaucannon

Market

Monticello Rd   Kenzo   5 miles

Hagen Road

Coombsville

This map extends from the northern edge of the City of Napa,
up through the remarkable Oak Knoll district past Yountville.
Oak Knoll is remarkable because they grow an amazing variety of high-quality grapes there. On the next two pages the
map is split for west (E2) and east (E3), and after that
are two maps of downtown Yountville.

Vine Cliff

Paraduxx

Yountville

Goosecross

Gemstone
Tom Scott

Kapcsandy

Poetry Inn

Yountville Crossroad
Cliff Lede

Robert Sinskey?
Sold 2023

Baldacci

Stags Leap

Shafer

Silverado

Quioxte

Stags Leap Winery

Taylor

Odette

Pine Ridge

Robinson

Realm

Stag's Leap Cellars

Regusci Family

Antica

Chimney Rock

Clos Du Val

The Caves at Soda Canyon

Oak Knoll

White Rock

Relic

Loma Vista

Oak Knoll Rd
James Cole

Signorello

Darioush

Hagafen

Black Stallion

Market

Seven Apart

William Hill

Ellman

Atlas Peak Rd

Reynolds

Krupp

Silverado Resort

Market

Burgess

Bread & Butter
Razi

Wetstone

Judd's Hill

Napa Tasting Barn
Del Dotto Caves

Hyde de Villaine

Beaucannon
Market
Bougetz

Jarvis

Kenzo

Milliken Creek Inn

Coombsville

The whole town of **Yountville** is about a mile long and half a mile wide. All the luxury hotels and attractions are on the few streets shown here with Washington Street being the main shopping avenue. The town little walking town is well served with sidewalks and a lovely collection of sculptures.

Yountville Restaurants & Tasting Rooms

Until the 1970's, downtown **Yountville** was a backwater filled with cheap bars. In 1970, the arrival of Domaine Chandon kicked off the town's journey towards being a famous foodie destination. Today, it's a picture-perfect mix of fine hotels, spectacular restaurants, excellent tasting rooms and unique shops, of the exact kind you want to visit when you've been tasting wine.

Oakville & Rutherford,
The Heart of in the Valley

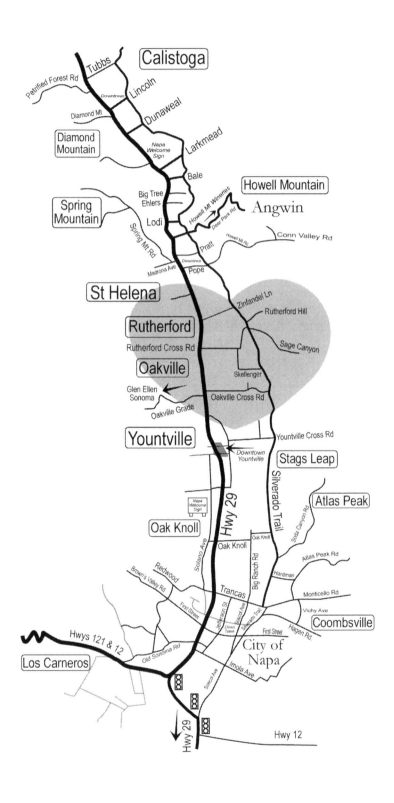

Oakville & Rutherford
West & East

See F3 for
the west side

See F4 for
the east side

For generations, **Oakville** and **Rutherford** were 'The Zone', the most desirable vineyard land, broad, flat, well drained, sunny and warm, but shaded from the punishing afternoon sunlight by the high mountains to the west. Today, it is filled with the vineyards of Napa's most famous brands, Robert Mondavi, Opus One, Silver Oak, Cakebread, Beaulieu Vineyards, Plumjack and Caymus just to name a few. Oakville Market serves as the 'downtown' of Oakville and the cluster of businesses around the Post Office makes up the slightly larger downtown of Rutherford. On the next pages, the map is split for west **(F3)** and east **(F4)**, followed by the map for Sage Canyon, Pritchard Hill, Chiles and Pope Valleys **(F5)**.

St. Helena

V. Sattui
Winery & Deli

North

Market
Flora Springs

Kelham

Ink Grade

Corison

Wheeler Farm

Napa Farmhouse Inn [H]

Del Dotto Winery Cave

Cathiard

Zinfandel Ln

Raymond

Whitehall Lane Winery

Sullivan   Fleury

Whitehall Lane

Prisoner

Tres Sabores   Pestoni

Bella Union

Galleron Rd

Mee Lane

Alpha Omega

Rutherford

Grgich Hills

Beaulieu

Caymus Inn

Rutherford Grill ➔ ®

[H]

Rutherford Rd

Inglenook

Elizabeth Spencer   Mathew Bruno   Market

Peju Province

La Luna Market & Taqueria

Staglin

Manley Ln

St Supery

Bella Oaks Ln

Foley Johnson

Sequoia Grove

One Hope

Cakebread

Turnbull

Robert Mondavi

Nickel & Nickel

Opus One

Saddleback

1881 Wine Merchant
Oakville

Groth

Market

Oakville

Oakville Cross Rd

Ghost Block

Silver Oak

Oakville Grade

Cardinale

Promontory
Futo

Far Niente

Gamble

Bond
Harlan

Welcome to Napa Sign

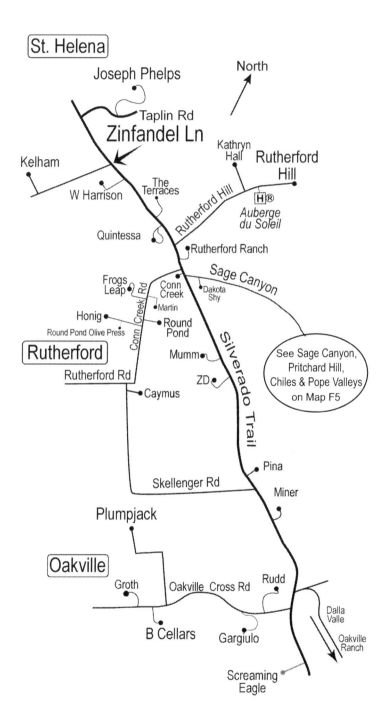

St. Helena

Joseph Phelps

North

Taplin Rd

Zinfandel Ln

Kathryn Hall

Rutherford Hill

Kelham

W Harrison

The Terraces

Rutherford Hill

H ®

Auberge du Soleil

Quintessa

Rutherford Ranch

Sage Canyon

Frogs Leap

Conn Creek Rd

Conn Creek

Dakota Shy

Honig

Martin

Round Pond Olive Press

Round Pond

Rutherford

Mumm

Silverado Trail

Rutherford Rd

ZD

See Sage Canyon, Pritchard Hill, Chiles & Pope Valleys on Map F5

Caymus

Pina

Skellenger Rd

Miner

Plumpjack

Oakville

Groth

Oakville Cross Rd

Rudd

Dalla Valle

B Cellars

Gargiulo

Oakville Ranch

Screaming Eagle

Sage Canyon, Pritchard Hill, Chiles & Pope Valleys

Good Advice: Every winery on this map is by appointment and has been that way for many years. When you are visiting, get their written directions to the winery. These are small, mountain roads through heavily wooded areas with very few landmarks or even numbers. We make the maps as accurate as possible but when navigating these hills, you need all the help you can get, plus extra time. Also, bring snacks and water because there is no place up here to buy food.

Saint Helena

See G2 for
the west side

Downtown
Map G5

See G3 for
the east side

As you travel north the valley narrows with the neck of the hourglass being the town of **St. Helena**. Many of the early investors who could afford the more expensive land settled close to downtown, so there is a concentration of wineries and wonderful buildings here. In the next two pages the map is split into west **(G2)** and east **(G3)**. Past that is a directory of hotels, restaurants and tasting rooms and a map of downtown St. Helena **(G4)**. This was always the fanciest up valley town, before Yountville was transformed into a foodie destination. In the hills to the east are the wineries of Howell Mountain **(Map I)**, and to the west are the wineries of Spring Mountain **(Map H)**.

23

West Saint Helena
Along Highway 29

See G5 for
Downtown
St. Helena

N

To Calistoga

Faust ● ■ Deer Park Rd

Culinary Institute
of America ®
Charles
● Krug

Beringer ●

Pratt Ave

St Helena

See Downtown Map

Sunshine
Market

Pope St

® Merryvale

Gott's Roadside ® ®

® Farmstead @ Long Meadow Ranch

• VGS Potelle   • Crocker Starr

Dowdell Ln

Clif Family ●

Davies ● Salvestrin ●

Chase
Cellars

Grayson Ave

Sulphur Springs Ave

Lewlling Ln

Louis M Martini ●

● Heitz

Sutter Home ●

Prager Port ●

Hall ● Press ®

Market

● V. Sattui

Taplin ●

Flora Springs ●

Ink Grade ●

Sinegal ●

Inglewood Ave

Young
Inglewood

● Corison

Wheeler ● Kelham
Farms ●

Zinfandel Lane

Cathiard ●

Napa Farmhouse Inn H

Dana
Estates ●

Del Dotto

● Raymond

● Sullivan ● Fleury

Prisoner ● Galleron Rd

Whitehall Lane ●

Ink House Inn H

Pestoni ●

Mee Lane

Whitehall Ln

S. Whitehall Ln

● Bella Union

Alpha
Omega ●

Tres
Sabores ●

Grgich
Hills ●

Rutherford

Beaulieu ●

Rutherford Grill ®

H Rancho
Caymus Inn

Ingelnook ●

Rutherford Rd

Elizabeth Mathew
Spencer   Bruno

To Calistoga

N

Deer Park Rd

Pratt Ave

Meadowood Resort

Napa Valley Reserve

See Downtown St Helena Map

Meadowood Ln

Seven Stones

Palladian

Pope St

St Helena

Silverado Trail

See Howell Mt Map for the Conn Valley Wineries

Howell Mt Rd

Auburn James

Joseph Phelps

Kelham

Zinfandel Road

Terraces

Denali Estate

W Harrison

Taplin Rd

Rutherford

Kathryn Hall

Rutherford Hill

Quintessa

Rutherford Ranch

Auberge du Soleil

Frog's Leap

Honig

Conn Creek

Sage Canyon

Rutherford Rd

Round Pond

Mumm

ZD

25

Saint Helena Hotels, Restaurants & Tasting Rooms

Hotels
Alila: Located at the north end of the downtown and owned by the Hyatt group. This is a luxury hotel with a great restaurant created on the site of a previous hotel.

The Southbridge Hotel: Located at the south end of the downtown, this charming boutique hotel shares its building with a restaurant. Across the way is a spa.

The Wydown Hotel: This charming downtown boutique Inn sits at the corner of Adams and Hwy 29 (St. Helena Highway). It was created in an older building.

Meadowood: This well-known luxury resort off the Silverado Trail, a five-minute drive from the downtown, is still rebuilding after the 2020 Glass Fire.

The Harvest Inn: This luxury hotel is a five-minute ride from the downtown on St. Helena Hwy with a nice restaurant.

Vineyard Country Inn: This is a small mid-priced Inn five minutes from the downtown.

El Bonita Motel: This is the most reasonable place to stay near downtown St. Helena. It's been there for many years.

Restaurants
1) Acacia House @ Alila Hotel (California)
2) Ana's Cantina (Bar Food)
3) Caffe Della Valle (European Style)
4) Charter Oak (California)
5) Cook (American)
6) Farmstead @ LMR (Farm to Table)
7) Gillwood's Cafe (Breakfast & Lunch)
8) Goose and Gander (American)
9) Gott's Roadside (Burgers)
10) The Harvest Table @ Harvest Inn (Farm to Table)
11) Himalayan Sherpa Kitchen (Nepalese)
12) Market (American)
13) Model Bakery
14) Napa Valley Roasters (Cafe)
15) Press (New American)
16) The Station (Breakfast & Lunch)
17) Tra Vigne Pizzeria
18) Villa Corona (Mexican)
19) The Gate House @ CIA (New American)

Wineries & Tasting Rooms
Merryvale Winery
Spottswode Winery
Salvestrin Winery
The Saint, Luxury Wine Lounge
Erosion Wine and Brewery
Orin Swift Tasting Room

Downtown Saint Helena
Along Highway 29

North

Faust

Ballentine

William Cole

Morlet

Markham

Deer Park Rd

Culinary Institute of America 19 Ⓡ

Charles Krug

Beringer

Pratt Ave.

Alila Hotel
Acacia House Restaurant 1 Ⓡ Ⓗ

Fulton Ln

Califia

Spottswode

Wydown Hotel Ⓗ
Fuel

Madrone Ave

14

Railroad Ave

Adams St

13
12 Ⓡ   Ⓡ 5

Hunt Ave

Oak St

Money Way

7 Ⓡ

2 Ⓑ   Ⓡ 11
Ⓡ 3
16 Ⓡ   Ⓡ 18
Fuel

Pope St.

Spring St

Goose & Gander Ⓡ 8

Southbridge Hotel Ⓗ

17 Ⓡ Ⓗ

Merryvale

Market

Gott's Roadside 9 Ⓡ

Ⓡ 4

6 Ⓡ

Farmstead @ Long Meadow Ranch

Crocker Starr

Mitchell Dr

Clif Family

VGS Potelle

Dowdell Ln

Davies

Salvestrin

Grayson Ave

Vineyard Country Inn Ⓗ
El Bonita Ⓗ

Louis M Martini

Sulphur Springs Ave

Harvest Inn 10 Ⓡ Ⓗ

Heitz

Lewlling Ln

Prager Port

Sutter Home

V. Sattui Winery & Deli

Hall

Press Ⓡ 15

Market

Rather than a mountain, this area is a series of ridges that allow cool air and fog from the Russian River Valley to flow through the canyons into the northern part of the Napa Valley. The top of **Spring Mountain** sits above the fog line so when the valley floor is covered with mist those elevated vineyards are soaking up the Sunshine. The wineries are all small family affairs except for Lokoya and Spring Mountain. Newton is located here but tastings are held elsewhere.

Do not use Howell Mt. Rd to go to the Howell Mt Wineries. It is a narrow dangerous road subject to closures. Only use it to go to the Conn Valley wineries.

Howell Mountain wines are famous for their big tannins and great aging potential. The mountain is a large volcanic ball that faces west, exposing the vineyards to the kind of strong after-noon sunlight that makes the vines extract sulfur from the soil. These are all small wineries tucked on mountain roads with the largest being the two Cade wineries owned by and Arkenstone.

As you travel north of St. Helena the valley floor rises and widens. This is the warmest part of the valley where farmers have grown heat-loving Zinfandel for generations and you will see those vineyards filled with their bush-like, 'headed' vines, that the Italians call 'Umbrello', for umbrella.

The top of the valley is capped by Mount St. Helena, an ancient volcano that blocks cold winds coming from the north. The town of **Calistoga** has an old west feeling, but it is filled with Hot Spring Spas, cute stores and tasting rooms.

Calistoga Attractions

Hotels:

Solage is a luxury resort on the Silverado Trail a short walk to downtown. It has all the luxury features including their wonderful Solbar restaurant.

The Four Seasons resort, residences and Truss restaurant and Elusa winery are across from Solage. Their only sign is the address, 400 Silverado Trail.

The Calistoga Motor Lodge and Spa has its own hot spring pools and its own trendy Fleetwod restaurant. The themed stylish rooms are smaller but a great deal.

Indian Springs Calistoga is the oldest and largest spa hotel and it continues to shine. Its Sam's Club Restaurant is very good, and the overall prices are medium high.

Dr. Wilkinson's Spa, a long-time fave, was recently upgraded adding their 'House of Better' restaurant.

Mount View Hotel & Spa is a very elegant art deco boutique hotel in the center of town on the main street.

Some of the other Hot Springs hotels include the **Roman Spa, the Upvalley Inn, Calistoga Spa, Golden Haven**. There are numerous great B&B's and cottages that range from luxury to affordable.

Restaurants

Calistoga Depot has a great deli, bar and seating.
Calistoga Inn Brewery sits alongside the river.
Cafe Sarafornia for breakfast and lunch.
Calistoga Roastery for the best coffee and quick bites.
Hydro Bar is great for burgers and light fare.
Evangeline for elegant downtown dining.
Sam Brannan Cottages has a cute cafe.
Buster's BBQ is a long-time favorite food stand.

Tasting Rooms

On Foothill Blvd just off Lincoln, are several excellent tasting rooms. The Tank Garage and Lola don't require appointments, but Rivers Marie and Mathew Wallace may. In the center of town on either side of the Napa River are Lawer, August Briggs, Maria Concetto, Olabisi, Vault, Romeo, Cami Art & Wine, Picayune Cellars & Mercantile and Somnium. Calistoga is mostly a casual collection of wine tasting rooms, restaurants, small hotels and unique shopping.

Downtown Calistoga

Calistoga is the northern-most town in Napa, and it has the feeling of the old west. Unlike the other valley towns, with locations that cater to tourists, it has a larger working-class population. It also has a wealth of small hotels and inns that offer lovely rooms at reasonable prices compared to much of Napa Valley. Because of the numerous hot springs that bubble to the surface here this has been a spa town since it was founded in the late 1800's. The railroad right-of-way that goes up the valley was established to bring guests up-valley to the local hotels. Beyond this being a wine destination, many people still come here to 'take the waters' which makes sense, since wine was the original health drink!

Napa American Viticulture Area Dates

Napa Valley: January 27 1981

Los Carneros: August 18, 1983

Howell Mountain: December 30, 1983

Wild Horse Valley: November 30, 1988

Stags Leap: January 27, 1989

Mt. Veeder: February 20, 1990

Atlas Peak: January 22, 1992

Spring Mountain: May 13, 1993

Oakville: July 2, 1993

Rutherford: July 2, 1993

St. Helena: September 11, 1995

Chiles Valley: February 17, 1999

Yountville: March 19, 1999

Diamond Mountain: June 1, 2001

Oak Knoll: February 25, 2004

Calistoga: December 8, 2009

Coombsville: December 14, 2011

Chapter 1: Getting Around Napa Valley

Napa and Sonoma are the world's two top wine tourism destinations. Napa is a third of the size of Sonoma and significantly warmer and sunnier, allowing them to grow more of the expensive Cabernet Sauvignon and its blending grapes, which fill sixty percent of their vineyards.

The valley is thirty miles long and, at its widest, five miles across. The valley floor is bordered on both sides by steep hills. At the base of the valley is the San Pablo Bay, with its cool Carneros winds, and nightly fogs, that support Chardonnay and Pinot Noir vineyards. As you go northwest up the valley it gets increasingly warmer.

At the town of Saint Helena, the valley narrows to a mile across. Farther north, it widens and gets even warmer around Calistoga at the foot of an ancient volcano called Mount Saint Helena. Beyondthe distinctive cone are Lake County to the northeast and Sonoma County to the northwest. Napa has been an important tourist destination since the late 1800's, originally for its hots springs and health spas.

It is a beautiful place and besides the wineries, of which there are about a eight hundred, the region has lovely hotels, restaurants, shopping, culinary programs, mud baths, horseback riding and lots of golf courses. The growing areas are divided into districts called 'American Viticulture Areas' or AVAs.

They describe growing regions that produce unique wine characteristics due to their climatic and geologic characters.

As of 2020 Napa has sixteen AVA's, ranging from cool **Los Carneros** at the base of the valley up to hot **Calistoga** at the top. Some AVAs include the rocky, basaltic **Mount Veeder** AVA in the southwest, volcanic **Howell Mountain** AVA in the northeast, the rustic **Wild Horse Valley** AVA in the southeast and in the northwest the breezy **Spring Mountain** AVA.

The variety of territories placed so close together is remarkable and in the middle of all of them are Oakville and Rutherford, two of the world's most famous wine growing locations and well-known AVAs.

The wide diversity is due to Napa's eclectic geological nature, which is more varied than most growing regions and its numerous climatic zones. That allows the local vintners to grow widely different grapes in a relatively small valley, one fifth the size of Bordeaux.

In the south near the bay, Napa grows the grapes of northern France (Burgundy and Champagne), in the center, it grows the grapes of southwest France (Bordeaux and Cahors) and at the peak of the valley, they grow the grapes of Sicily.

Navigation Tip: Watch for the small white on blue winery signs (one foot high by three feet wide) placed at eye level at the side of the road. They are often the only signs that announce the winery before their entrance. They are also sometimes used to mark hotels.

Navigating the Main Roads Easily

Because it is relatively small, getting around Napa is easy. *The valley roads are laid out like a ladder. Highway 29 (St Helena Highway) and the Silverado Trail are the ladder's uprights, going from the southeast to the northwest.* Between them is the Napa River, which has its sources near Mount Saint Helena, running south the length of the valley through the city of Napa, and emptying into the San Pablo Bay at the city of Vallejo. Highway 29 is the 'main road' that connects the downtowns and has a few different names along its route. It parallels the tracks of the Wine Train, a tourist attraction that uses a right-of-way established in the late 1800's, to bring tourists to Sam Brannan's Calistoga Hot Springs. The Silverado Trail began as the Wappo tribe's trading trail that wound through the eastern hills to avoid the flooded valley floor during the winter rainy season.

These two 'upright' roads are connected, east to west, about every mile, by bridges and crossroads that form the 'rungs' of the ladder. Heading north, these roads begin with *Trancas Street*, which is the northern commercial edge of the city of Napa. The next three are *Yountville Cross Road, Oakville Cross Road and Rutherford Road* which are each named for their towns. Note: *Rutherford starts at Hwy 29 and then splits into Conn Creek Road and Skellenger Lane* with both making the final connections to the Silverado Trail.

Next are the crossroads for the town of Saint Helena; *Zinfandel Lane, Pope Street, Pratt Avenue, Deer Park Road*, (which continues up the hill to Howell Mountain and the town of Angwin) *Lodi Lane and Bale Lane*. In the northernmost part of the valley the crossroads of the town of Calistoga are *Larkmead Lane, Dunaweal Lane, Lincoln Avenue and Tubbs Lane.* The latter was named for the founder of the winery that is now Chateau Montelena, Alfred Tubbs.

Both Chateau Montelena and Calistoga's Old Faithful Geyser are located on Tubbs Lane and from the Silverado Trail end it meets the route that begins a steep climb up Mount Saint Helena into Lake County. From the other end, you can connect to the road the brings you north, over the hills, into Sonoma's popular Alexander Valley.

While Highway 29 is home to most of the oldest wineries, many very interesting wineries make their homes on the crossroads and the 'Trail'. For example, you'll find Cliff Lede on Yountville Cross Road, Silver Oak, Groth, B Cellars and Plumpjack are all on Oakville Cross Road. Caymus, Frog's Leap, and Round Pound arhe on Rutherford Road or the connecting Conn Creek Road, and Kelham Family is on Zinfandel Lane. North of Saint Helena, Duckhorn is at the corner of Silverado and Lodi Lane, notably the shortest crossroad.

I**n Northern Napa, many of the biggest wineries are on the crossroads;** Frank Family and Larkmead Vineyards are on Larkmead Lane (the former Family Estate of Lillie Coit, as in Coit Tower in San Francisco. Sterling (famous for its tramway), Clo Pegase and Girard are all on Dunaweal Lane, while Chateau Montelena, and Tamber Bey are on Tubbs Lane, which is the furthest north crossroad that connects Highway 29 to the Silverado Trail.

A perfect example of the Silverado Trail's importance is the Stags Leap AVA in the southeast corner of the valley. The Trail, along a short stretch of road, bisects about twenty well known and, in some cases, prestigious wineries including Shafer, Stag's Leap Cellars, Silverado Vineyards, Chimney Rock, Pine Ridge, Realm and Quixote.

Warning: *Some roads don't cross between Hwy 29 and the Silverado Trail, so check the maps.* The great thing about this road arrangement is that it makes it possible to travel from winery to winery by only making right turns which is both safer and faster on busy days. This is helpful in a place where people routinely drink alcohol and get behind the wheel.

Clusters of Wineries

The oldest wineries were located along Highway 29, giving them easy access to the main road and the train tracks for moving wagons full of grapes and wine. The oldest stone wineries like Far Niente, Inglenook, Beringer and Christian Brothers, now the CIA Saint Helena campus, were built into small hillsides. This served their gravity-fed design which sent the grape wagons up the slope to the powerfully built second floor where the grapes were unloaded into the fermentation tanks. When the wine was ready to go into the aging barrels, a valve was opened and gravity carried the juice through a hose to the barrels on the floor below, where they were rolled into the adjacent cave.

As you drive north on Highway 29 there are areas where the vineyards sit edge to edge. In the 1960's and 70's, when there were only about twenty wineries, the most popular were on the north bound side of the narrow road to better catch customers coming up from the towns around the bay.

Tastings were free and visitors would go into the wineries on the right side of the road all the way to Charles Krug, just north of Saint Helena. Then they would cross the street and visit Christian Brothers for one more tasting before heading home. This was a great strategy on a narrow road with questionable shoulders and lots of drunks.

This brings us to a story. The modern Robert Mondavi Winery was started in the 1960's and it is on the south bound, left side of the road. Mondavi's new winery would be among the first visitors would see, which could be great for business if he could convince people to stop on their way up valley. By the time they were heading south they already had enough wine in them. Even though there was available land on the north bound side of the road, he wanted the renowned To Kalon vineyard, on the south bound side.

He was aiming to make world class wines, and this western slope is where many of Napa's historically important Oakville and Rutherford vineyards are found. It is well drained, rocky bench land that is shaded in the late afternoon by Mount St. John, protecting the vines from the punishing western sunshine. But, what's best for the grapes wasn't as good for getting customers in the door, so Bob Mondavi used some innovative 'tricks' to get people into his new winery and onto his tours.

Then as now, on weekend mornings traffic north on Highway 29 can be heavy. He would have his son Michael drive his car up from downtown Napa and then sit in the road with this turn signal on, while cars stacked up behind him. Someone, maybe Bob, would be holding up a sign that said, 'Free Tours and Wine' and waving people in. When Michael relented and made the turn, some cars would typically follow him. He would park, jump out of the car and walk the visitors into the tasting room. Then he would head downtown again.

There is more traffic on Hwy 29 than ever before, and the town of Saint Helena is a north-bound bottleneck. *If you are going up valley past the town, bypass the congestion by taking the Silverado Trail north.* It is often clear sailing from Trancas Street, all the way to Calistoga. If you are going up Hwy 29 and want to miss the bottleneck, Zinfandel Lane is the last crossroad you can take over to the Silverado Trail. At the end of the day southbound traffic backs up in

Rutherford and Oakville, more often on Highway 29, but less often on the Trail. There is a wonderful group of wineries on the Silverado Trail in the south part of valley in the Oak Knoll and Stags Leap districts, but north of Yountville Cross Road the Trail wineries are spread out.

Chapter 2: Quick ABC's for Tasting Wine

The way you drink wine with a meal is different from how you sample it in a tasting room. The funny techniques you see people using during tastings help them perceive the wine better through the senses of sight, scent and taste. It starts with the glassware. Wineries use crystal goblets because they are rougher than glass. When you swirl the wine, those microscopic bumps pull apart its molecules, mixing them with oxygen, releasing the aromas and flavors for you to experience. Hold the glass by the stem because that makes it easier to move the wine around inside the glass. Fancier wineries have fancier glasses.

Start by holding the glass upright and taking a sniff. Much of what you're smelling is alcohol rising off the liquid. Next, set the glass on the tabletop, place your fingers firmly on top of the base and vigorously swirl the wine. Now, pick the glass up and hold it at a 45-degree angle and put your nose on the glass' lower lip, and take a sniff.

Because the alcohol fumes are rising in the globe and slipping out the upper edge, bypassing your nose, you're smelling the pure fruit flavors below, the wonderful scent of fermented grapes! Sip the wine and move it around your mouth, so it touches all your taste buds from the tip of your tongue to the valley in its center, and then, both sides.

Once the flavors are well dispersed, swallow the sip. Repeat this process until there is none left. Note that there are scent notes that are only released when they touch your tongue. To access them, gently breathe in through your mouth so the aromas on your palate reach your nose via the back of your throat. There is another quality you should note called 'mouth feel'. It is how the texture of the wine feels to the surface of your mouth. Is it sharply acidic, soothingly silky, or almost sticky and syrupy? One 'mouth feel' to watch out for is the almost flame-like touch of a high alcohol, dry wine, which is why that kind of wine is called 'hot'.

Port is also high in alcohol, but the wine is heavy and sweet, so the alcohol is deeply embedded in the flavors. But, many Zinfandels and Cabernets are very hot, at 15% to 16% alcohol, while dry (meaning that all the grape sugar has been converted to alcohol). If the dehydrating alcohol is not well moderated and integrated into the wine, it will feel like a sip dries out your tongue and you may be thirstier after the tasting than before you began. With those wines the alcohol may have been concentrated on the surface by the swirling. You may be able to fix that by holding the glass almost horizontally and gently rolling it for twenty or thirty seconds. This may help re-integrate the alcohol into the liquid and soften the mouth feel.

Wine Geek Alert! There is an odd phenomenon that happens with wines that have been aged in oak for an extended period, usually eighteen months or more. As related to me by winemakers, when you swirl the wine clockwise you will smell predominantly fruit flavors. But when you swirl counterclockwise, you will also notice the nutty, sometimes spicy flavors that come from the barrel. Why does this happen? According to Ralph's best quasi-scientific analysis, it is due to the relative efficiency of vortices. A clockwise swirl more efficiently mixes the various part of the wine together. But the less efficient counterclockwise swirl allows the layers to separate. The wooden barrel flavors are the last ones to be infused into the juice and in this less organized mix, some of those woody notes are left floating at the top for your nose to discover. This technique is used by some winemakers to determine a barrel's influence on the wine. If you have a good sense of smell, you will notice the difference. Now you are officially a Wine Geek!

Chapter 3: Napa Winery Directory

Ackerman Family – Downtown Napa tasting from Coombsville Vineyards – Cabernet Sauvignon, Sauvignon Blanc, Blends – 608 Randolph St, Napa, CA 94559 – www.ackermanfamilyvineyards. com (855) 238–9463 – Their tastings and seminars are conducted in a beautifully restored Queen Anne Victorian mansion in downtown Napa. Map A2. Does not appear on map.

Acumen Napa Valley – Downtown Napa Tasting Room – Wines: Bordeaux and Burgundy – 1315 First Street, Napa 94558 – www.acumenwine.com – (707) 492–8336 – Hours: 10:00 am – 7:00pm, closed Tues and Wed – Their vineyards are on the difficult to access Atlas peak region, which explains why a downtown tasting room was the smarter solution. Map A2. Does not appear on map.

Adamvs Winery – Ultra-Premium Howell Mountain – Wines: Cabernet Sauvignon, Merlot, Blends – 555 College Rd Angwin CA 94508 www.adamvs.com – (707) 965–0555 – Hours: 9:00am – 5:00pm – This is an ultra–premium winery on the site of the old White Cottage Vineyards. They farm their land using the Biodynamic method, the highest form of organic. The wines are big and benefit from aging, because the Howell Mountain soils are thin and sit on top of a massive volcanic ball. The tasting space is as much a piece of art as it is a building. Map I

Allora Vineyards – Small Family Winery – Wines: Cabernet Sauvignon, Petite Syrah – 3244 Ehlers Lane Saint Helena CA 94574 – www.alloravineyards.com – (707) 963–6071 – This is a small family winery where the barrel room and comfortable tasting room are below the beautiful house. The tasting is normally done by the family and their production is small, so they sell out quickly. Map J

43

Alpha Omega – Fun, delicious experience – Wines: Bordeaux and Burgundy – 1155 Mee Lane Saint Helena CA 94574 – www.aowinery.com – (707) 963–9999 – Hours: 10:00am – 6:00pm – This is powerhouse winery, on a side street just off Highway 29, from which you can see their fountains soaring into the sky. When you sit outside on the tasting patio, you find yourself enjoying the cooling spray, now and then, if the wind comes from the correct quarter. They make wonderful wines, with a fantastic staff and the place is a lot of fun. They have both a tasting bar and seated tastings outside on the patio, which is the preferred experience. Map G2. They also have a tasting room in downtown Napa. Map A2, Zone 1, Does not appear on map.

Altamura Winery – Wooden Valley – Wines: Cabernet Sauvignon, Sangiovese – 1700 Wooden Valley Road Napa CA 94558 – www.altamura.com – (707) 253–2000 – Hours: Appointment – They are a premium wine maker with long ties to the Valley and a great reputation, producing about 5000 cases yearly. Their 400–acre property is located nine miles east from downtown Napa in an area with no other wineries. They are off the beaten path on the narrow, mountain route between Napa and Suisun Valley in Solano County, which has its own wonderful collection of small, reasonably priced family wineries. Does not appear on map.

Amici Cellars – Small in the Calistoga Hills – Wines: Cabernet Sauvignon, Pinot Noir, Chardonnay – 3130 Old Lawley Toll Road Calistoga, CA 94515 – www.amicicellars.com – (707) 967–9560 – Hours: Appointment – This is the hot part of the valley, but they source grapes from various regions and produce a wide selection of Cabernets. These are small lots of high scoring wines that are reasonably priced. They are in on the foothills of the Palisades to the east of downtown Calistoga. Map K

Amizetta Vineyard –A Long Drive to beautiful destination in the eastern mountains – Wines: Cabernet Sauvignon and Blends – 1099 Greenfield Road Saint Helena CA 94574 – www.amizetta.com – (707) 963–1460 – Hours: 10:00am – 4:00pm Appointment – They are 6.1 miles from Silverado Trail at the eastern edge of the Napa Valley. This is a small winery and the family lives on the property. When you make the appointment make sure they give you instructions because it is not easy to find and there is a gate, so you may need the code. These are narrow roads and the drive up to the winery must be taken SLOWLY, so allow extra time to get there. But it is worth the ride because the tasting is usually conducted outside on their expansive patio, that sits at about 1000 feet elevation, with great views of the hillsides and Lake Hennessey. Map I

Amulet Winery formerly Tuck Beckstoffer – Collectors – Wines: Bordeaux and Burgundy 230 North Fork Crystal Springs Road Saint Helena, CA 94574 www.amuletestate.com – (707) 200–4410 – Hours: Appointment – Map J

Ancien Wines – Coombsville– Small with grapes from distant vineyards – Wines: Burgundy – East Napa, Ca 94581 – www.ancien-wines.com – (707) 927–6594 – Hours: Appointment – Call for directions – They are an exception in warm Coombsville because they specialize in the cool weather grapes, Pinot Noir and Chardonnay. That is because their vineyards are no place nearby. They source grapes from places where these grapes thrive, Sonoma, the Central Coast and Washington State. They do a low–key tasting, in a little place that is not at all fancy but relaxed with good wines. Map D

Anderson's Conn Valley Vineyards – Caves in the Eastern Hills
Wines: Cabernet Sauvignon, Pinot Noir, Chardonnay – 680 Rossi Road Saint Helena CA 94574 – www.connvalleyvineyards.com – (707) 963–8600 – Hours: Appointment – They are 15 minutes from the Silverado Trail, up narrow winding roads, through low rolling hills to the east of the main valley. The tasting often includes a tour of the caves. It is a beautiful, off the beaten track location. Map I

Anomaly Vineyards – Saint Helena – Small for Collectors – Wines: Cabernet Sauvignon, Bordeaux Blend – P.O. Box 741. Saint Helena CA 94574 (Call for directions) – www.anomalyvineyards.com – (707) 967–8448 – Hours: 10:00am – 4pm, Monday–Saturday Appointment – This tiny winery is conveniently located at the western edge of the town of Saint Helena on a residential street, with vines across the way. The tasting is in the cellar below the little tower style winery. The wines are priced for collectors. This was retirement project for the owners, and it is well–managed and enjoyable. Does not appear on map.

Antica Napa Valley – Antinori Family, a long ride up Soda Canyon – Bordeaux and Burgundy – 3700 Soda Canyon Road Napa, CA 94558 www.anticanapavalley.com – (707)–257–8700 Ext. 1 – Hours: Appointment – Tours – This is a large winery with older caves at the far end of the narrow, winding Soda Canyon Road, so allow extra time to get there. The winery was built years ago originally as a joint venture, but eventually, the Antinori family of Tuscany, took control and they have developed the tasting experience. What it lacks in convenience it makes up for in natural beauty. Map E3

Aonair Winery – In the Eastern Hills of Conn Valley with Great Views – 647 Greenfield Rd. Saint Helena CA – www.aonairwine.com – (707) 738-8352 – This is a small and charming family winery that is a favorite of our clients. The scenic ride winds its way up into the eastern hills, so plan extra time to get there. The wines are wonderful and the hospitality is relaxed. Aonair is Gaelic for 'One Man', which describes the job of the winemaker. Navigation Tip: First, the turn off Conn Valley Rd. onto Greenfield Rd. is heavily wooded and the signs are not obvious so take your time. Second, the only sign at the winery is the address on the left side at a curve. The driveway drops steeply to the left so you won't see the winery from the road. Map I

Arcudi Wines – For Collectors – Wines: Bordeaux Blends – 83 1st St, Napa, CA 94559 – www.arcudiwines.com. Does not appear on map.

Artesa Winery – Spectacular View in Carneros – Wines: Burgundy, Bordeaux and Spanish – 1345 Henry Road Napa 94559 www.artesawinery.com – (707) 224–1668 – Hours: 10am –5pm Appointment for the seated tastings – They also have vineyards in Sonoma's Alexander Valley. This is a destination winery with spectacular views of Carneros and the San Pablo Bay. It was built by a Spanish wine making family. They removed the top of a hill, built the winery and replaced the top with the winery inside. It has stunning architecture, glass sculptures and splendid fountains. The spacious tasting room becomes a fun bar scene on the weekends, and there is plenty of room to spread out. There is a separate area and a patio for seated tastings. Take the tour of the caves and winery beneath your feet because it is worth seeing. From the patio you can see the DeRosa Art Preserve and the Domaine Carneros Winery. If you sit on Artesa's patio with your darling and a glass of wine, and that does not make you feel romantic, you are not doing it right. Map C

Arkenstone Vineyards – Howell Mountain – Wines: Estate Red, Syrah, Sauvignon Blanc – 335 West Lane Angwin, CA 94508 – www.arkenstone.com – (707) 965–1020 – Hours: Appointment – They schedule a limited number of Appointment for small groups. They are located down a side road. If you expect a rustic experience, which is common on Howell Mountain, not so much. Their main tasting lounge is modern, and the winery is an industrial style cave complex where numerous wine labels are made that is worth seeing. Map I

Arrow and Branch – Oak Knoll – Wines: Rose, Bordeaux Blends – 5215 Solano Ave. Napa CA 94558 – www.arrowandbranch.com – (707) 200–3640 Hours: Appointment – Culinary Wine pairing – Sourced from numerous prestigious Napa vineyards and tasted at their new winery just off Hwy 29. The wines are made by Phillipe Melka, a well known French born winemaker. This was started by whose sons have entered the business, and while they produce small lots the wine they are very high end. Their new location is wonderfully convenient only five minutes outside downtown, Map E2

Ashes and Diamonds – 4130 Howard Ln, Napa, CA 94558 (707) 666–4777– Hours: 11:00am – 7:00pm Appointment – www.ashesdiamonds.com – Wines: Bordeaux and Burgundy They are located just north of the city of Napa on the same driveway as the restaurant Don Giovanni. Because they are outside the agricultural Peserve, they can stay open later and serve food on the weekends. This was designed for the Millennial generation, stylish, big windows, minimalistic with open, social spaces and the wines are made in that palate. Map E2

Auburn James – Silverado Trail – Bordeaux and Burgundy - 1001 Silverado Trail South, Saint Helena CA 94574 – (707) 967–9100 www.auburnjames.com –– Hours 10:00am to 4:00pm Appointment – Bocce court – This is a located on a quick bend on the Silverado Trail. Its location makes it a bit hard to access, so when you visit consult the n detail and slow down well in advance of their driveway. This is a partnership between two winemakers who primarily focus on what they want to produce for their wine club. It is a pretty property tucked below the road's grade. Map G3

AXR Napa Valley – Tasting Room – Wines: Bordeaux Blends 3199 St Helena Highway North, Saint Helena, CA 94574 – www.axrnapavalley.com (707) 302–8181 – Hours: 10:00 am – 4:00 pm Appointment – This little tasting cottage north of Saint Helena has become quite popular thanks in part to a great winemaker. Map J

B Cellars – Oakville Hospitality – Wines: Bordeaux Style – 703 Oakville Cross Rd, Napa, CA 94558 – www.bcellars.com – (707) 709–8787 – 10:00am – 5:00pm Appointment – Tours – Culinary Pairings – Oakville is the heart of the Valley and B Cellars made their home on an old horse ranch. The design is sleek and created for hospitality, built around a commercial kitchen that makes food pairings. They have lovely grounds with playful, figurative sculptures. Their tours include their caves, which were designed for events. Map F4

Back Stage Vineyards – Oak Knoll District Family Winery – Wines: Cabernet Sauvignon, Pinot Noir, Chardonnay – 4162 Big Ranch Rd, Napa, CA 94558 – www.backstagewines.com – (707) 637-4030 – Hours: 10:00am – 5:00pm Appointment – This is new facility and tasting room for a winery that has been making wine and pouring it at their other tasting rooms in the bay area. High quality from small vineyards. Map E2

Baldacci Vineyards – Stags Leap District Family Winery – Wines: Cabernet Sauvignon, Pinot Noir – 6236 Silverado Trail Napa CA 94558 – www.baldaccivineyards.com – (707) 944–9261 – Hours: 10:00am – 5:00pm Appointment – This family–run winery is tucked into a southern facing hillside, surrounded by some of Napa's most famous labels. In 2021 they expanded their caves and built a new hospitality building. Map E3

Ballentine Vineyards – Wines: Cabernet Sauvignon, Chenin Blanc, Zinfandel, Merlot, Cabernet Franc, Syrah, Petite Syrah, Petit Verdot – 2820 St Helena Highway North Saint Helena CA 94574 – www.ballentinevineyards.com – (707) 963–7919 – Hours: 10:00am – 4:00pm Appointment – This fourth generation family vineyards and winery is under stated, but they make good value wines from their own grapes and pour them in a cute, compact tasting room on their patio overlooking their vineyards. The sign is primarily visible as you are traveling north. Map J

Barnett Vineyards – Premium Spring Mountain Views – Wines: Cabernet Sauvignon, Pinot Noir, Chardonnay – 4070 Spring Mountain Road Saint Helena CA 94574 – www.barnettvineyards.com – (707) 963–7075 – Hours: 10:00am – 4:00pm Appointment – A charming, family winery clinging to the side of Spring Mountain with incredible views from the tasting patios built into the hillside. Plan well in advance. Map H

Beaucanon Estate – Wines: Bordeaux and Burgundy – 1006 Monticello Road, Napa – www.beaucanonestate.com – (707) 254–1460 Hours: 10:00am – 4:00pm Appointment – Wines: Cabernet blends and Chardonnay. The Longwood Ranch vineyards owned by the Bordeaux de Conick family, was part of Salvador Vallejo's 1850's land grant. They have been making good quality, reasonably priced wine there for twenty years. They do limited tastings and can be hard to reach. Map E3

Beaulieu Vineyard – Grand Rutherford Winery – Wines: Cabernet Sauvignon, Chardonnay, Pinot Noir, Merlot, Zinfandel, Syrah, Sauvignon Blanc, Shiraz, Sangiovese, Viognier, Port, Blends – 1960 St Helena Highway (Highway 29). Rutherford 94559 – www.bvwines.com – (707) 967–5230 – Hours: 10:00am – 5:00pm – This is one of Napa's grand old wineries that survived Prohibition, thanks to the owner, Georges de Latour, providing sacramental wines to the Catholic churches thanks to his friend, the Archbishop of San Francisco. Prohibition was wonderful for church membership and the winery expanded to a million cases a year over that thirteen–year period. French for 'What a beautiful place', describes the original winery location across from Frog's Leap. They make both good value and premium wines. The main tasting room offers a wide line of wines, while the Reserve building, with its patio, pours the revered George de La Tour Reserve, produced since 1936. The reserve was started by Andre Tchelistcheff, the source of many winemaking innovations used internationally today. That is his statue outside the reserve room. Known as 'BV'. Map F3

Bell Wine Cellars – Fine Wines by Yountville – Wines: Cabernet Sauvignon, Syrah, Port, Chardonnay, Zinfandel, Viognier, Merlot, Sauvignon Blanc. 6200 Washington Street Yountville CA 94599 – www.bellwine.com – (707) 944–1673 – Hours: 10:30am to 4:00pm Appointment – This is a small, respected winery south of Yountville. The tasting is in the winery tank room or seated in one of the side rooms. The tour includes the vineyards and winery. They have a loyal clientele so much of their wine is shipped directly to their customers. The grounds are nice although mostly intended for the use of the wine club during events. Map E2

Bella Union – The New Label From Far Niente in the building that previously housed Provenance – Wines: Cabernet Sauvignon Blends

– 1695 St. Helena Highway S. – www.bellaunionwinery.farniente.com – (707) 967-9500 – Check Website for more information. Part of the Nickel family. F3

Benessere – Italian Varietals North of Saint Helena – Wines: Pinot Grigio, Sangiovese, Syrah, Zinfandel, Pinot Noir, Muscat di Canelli, Super Tuscan style – 1010 Big Tree Road Saint Helena CA 94574 – www.benesserevineyards.com – (707) 963–5853 Ext 105 – Hours: 10:00am – 5:00pm –This was founded by people who had a love of all things Italian. The name means 'Well Being' in Italian and between the beautiful location, the intimate tasting room and the wonderfully made wines that describes the place quite well. Map J

Bennett Lane Winery – Calistoga and Worth the Ride – Navigation Tip: Their driveway is located on Highway 128, not on Bennett Lane – Wines: Chardonnay, Cabernet Sauvignon, Blends 3340 Highway 128 Calistoga CA 94515 – www.bennettlane.com (707) 942–6684 Hours: 10:00am – 5:30pm – They are at the northern tip of the Napa Valley. Besides good wines, they also have picnic tables, good views and tours that include a demonstration vineyard. Their signature wine is called Maximus after the Roman Emperor Magnus Maximus. Map K

Beringer Vineyards – Saint Helena – History & Multiple Tours Wines: A wide variety ranging from commercial up to pricey 2000 Main Street Saint Helena 94574 – www.beringer.com (707) 967–4412 – Hours: 10am–6pm (10am – 5pm winter) Beringer is located at the north edge of downtown Saint Helena. It is one of the world's most visited wineries, but it is so spread out that it rarely feels crowded. Continuously in operation since in 1876, today the dramatic Rhine House that you can you see from the road hosts the reserve tasting, while the old winery building, hosts the general tasting and gift shop. The modern winery is across the street. They offer a wide variety of wines and tours. The most charming tasting experience is the reserve, because the building is gorgeous, patterned after the family home in Germany. Many of these Mansion wines are sold only at the winery, so if you think of Beringer as 'white Zinfandel', be prepared to have that idea knocked out of the park. Map J

Blackbird Vineyards – Oak Knoll Merlot tasted in the Crusher District, Wines: Bordeaux and Burgundy – 831 Latour Court, Suite B1 Napa – www.blackbirdvineyards.com – (707) 252–4444 – Hours: Appointment – The vineyards are located at Big Ranch Road and Oak Knoll Cross Road. Their name comes from the local patois in France, where Merlot means blackbird. Map A1. In the Corporate Park. Does not appear on map.

Black Cat Vineyard – Coombsville – Wines: Syrah, Cabernet Sauvignon, Zinfandel – 1352 4th Ave, Napa, CA 94559 – www.blackcatvineyard.com – (707) 321–0866 – This is a small family winery where the owner is the winemaker. She makes beautiful wines. Their own Coombsville estate vineyards were planted in the late 90's, to Syrah and Cabernet Sauvignon. But they also source fruit from vineyards in Rutherford and Howell Mountain. Map D

Black Stallion Winery – Southern Silverado Trail – Wines: Chardonnay, Pinot Grigio, Sauvignon Blanc, Muscat Canelli, Rose', Merlot, Syrah, Cabernet Sauvignon – 4089 Silverado Trail Napa CA 94558 www.blackstallionwinery.com – (707) 253–1400 – Hours: 10:00am 5:00pm – This stone building was previously an equestrian center which explains the statue at the entrance. They are conveniently located on the southern edge of the Silverado Trail minutes north of downtown Napa. They have a spacious, beautifully appointed tasting room, including wonderful seating areas for special tastings and a comfy room just for the wine club. To the side they have a spacious outdoor tasting area complete with a bar. Nearby are the Reynolds Family winery, Darioush and Luna. Navigation Tip: Enter by the driveway directly in front of the winery because it is more dramatic. That brings you around to the back where you will find the entrance. Map E3

Blankiet Estate – Stunning Yountville Estate – 2358 California Dr, Yountville, CA 94599 – www.blankiet.com – (707) 963–2001 – Appointment – This hillside estate sits above the Dominus vineyards on the Mayacamas mountain slopes. It is directly east of downtown Yountville. This is an elegant property in a building that resembles a French castle. The caves and tasting room are classic. The only challenge is that their production does not equal the demand, so the wine is available via their waiting list. With that said, the property is so special that it is well worth the visit. Map E2

Blue Oak – Coombsville Collectors – Wines: Chardonnay, Merlot and a Bordeaux Blend – 44 Blue Oak Ln, Napa, CA 94558 – www.blueoakvineyard.com – (707) 253–1382 – This is a little vineyard that produces high quality wines that are reasonably priced compared to some of their neighbors. Because of the combination of prices and quality the wines are mostly available by allotment. They do not do many tastings, but for the collector this is a good place to visit. Map D

Boeschen Vineyards – Saint Helena – Wines: Bordeaux Blends 3242 Silverado Trail North Saint Helena, CA 94574 www.boeschenvineyards.com – (707) 963–3674 – Hours: 10:00 am – 3:30pm Appointment – The classic Bordeaux grapes including a Petite Verdot. The location is pretty and doing the tasting with the wine maker is always special. They do limited tastings so schedule well in advance. They are south of Rombauer and Failla. Map J

Boich Family Cellar – for Collectors – Wines: Bordeaux – 651 Wall Rd, Napa, CA 94558 –www.boichfamilycellar.com – (707) 254–8500 Hours: Appointment – At Hunnicutt. Map J

Bouchaine Vineyards – Carneros Views – Wines: Chardonnay, Pinot Noir, Pinot Gris, Syrah, Pinot Meunier, Gewürztraminer 1075 Buchli Station Road Napa CA 94559 – www.bouchaine.com – (707) 252–9065 – Hours: 10:30 – 5:00pm Appointment. This is one of the jewels of Los Carneros. In 2019 they opened a new hospitality building overlooking the original tasting room, which they continue to use for walk–in tastings. The wines are elegantly made, and you should visit early in the day when your taste buds are fresh. Once you taste big Napa Cabernets your palate will be too saturated to appreciate the subtle flavors of Pinot and Chardonnay. Map C

Bounty Hunter Bar and Restaurant – 975 1st St, Napa, CA 94559 Wines: A wide variety – www.bountyhunterwinebar.com – We've included this because it is more than just a bar, they also produce their own wines. They offer an amazing array of wines by the glass, so you can taste many of the local standouts. They also have a fun menu that goes well with wine. It is in downtown Napa near the corner of First and Main. Map A2 Zone 2 Does not appear on map.

Boyd Family Vineyards – Oak Knoll – Wines: A wide variety including a great Rose – 4042 Big Ranch Road, Napa CA 94558 – www.boydwine.com – (707) 254–7353 – This is a small family winery that mostly sells their wine via the web and to their wine club. The wines are high quality and reasonably priced. They are next door to the Biale winery by the intersection of Salvador Avenue and Big Ranch Road. They are not normally open to visits but if you are interested in their wines give them a call next time you are in the valley. Map E2

Brand Napa Valley – Sage Canyon Collectors – Wines: Bordeaux Blends – 90 Long Ranch Rd, St Helena, CA 94574 – www.brand-napavalley.com – (707) 963–1199 – Hours: Appointment This is an premium winery at a bend of the road up to the ridge that overlooks the valley. The hospitality space is gracious and done in a western theme, complete with saddles and horseshoes, hence brand! When you arrive, they open the. Map F5

Brasswood Cellars – Food, Wine and Events in Saint Helena - 3111 Saint Helena Highway North, Saint Helena, CA 94574 – www.brasswood.com (707) 968–5434 – Hours: 10:00am – 5:00pm – Bar and Restaurant: 11:30am – 9:00pm – Cafe Market and Bakery: 9:00am – 5:00pm. Unlike most Napa wineries they can have food and a winery together because they are in a commercial zone. So, they have all the features of V. Sattui, without the crazy crowds because they are north of downtown Saint Helena. Their own wines are good and reasonably priced. Their winery is a custom crush facility that serves small labels, that are poured in the facility's tasting areas. Map J

Bravante Vineyards – Howell Mountain Cave Tasting – Wines: Bordeaux – 300 Stone Ridge Road Angwin CA – www.bravantevineyards.com – (707) 965–2552 – Hours: Appt. Map I

Bread and Butter – 3105 Silverado Trail, Napa, CA 94558 – www.breadandbutterwines.com – (833) 332-7323 – This large production winery opened a new premium tasting room in 2021 on the southern edge of the Silverado Trail. They are using local grapes and a local winemaker. It is convenient and the wines are well made and priced. Map E3

Bremer Family Winery – Deer Park Appointment – Wines: Cabernet Sauvignon, Merlot, Zinfandel, Cabernet Franc, Claret, Petite Syrah, Port, White Port – 975 Deer Park Road Saint Helena CA 94574 – www.bremerfamilywinery.com – (707) 963–5411 – Hours: 10:00am to 5:00pm – They are tucked on the hillside of Howell Mountain. The tastings are mostly either on the patio or in the winery depending on the weather. It is low key with good wines. The old wine building was restored and tied into their newer caves. Map I

Brian Arden Wines – 331 Silverado Trail N, Calistoga, CA 94515 (707) 942–4767 – Hours: 11:00am – 4:30pm Appointment – www.brianardenwines.com – While they are located on the Silverado Trail, they are inside the Calistoga city limits. The family are grape growers in Lake County. They make lovely wines and pour them in a modern setting designed for relaxing. Map K

Brown Estate – Downtown Napa Tasting Room – Wines: Bordeaux, General French Blends – 1005 Coombs Street Napa CA – www.brownestate.com – (707) 963–2435 – Hours: Appointment 11:00am – 7:00pm – Estate Tours for members. Map A2 Zone 1 Does not appear on map.

Buehler Vineyards – Conn Valley Appointment – Wines: Cabernet Sauvignon, Chardonnay, Zinfandel, White Zinfandel - 820 Greenfield Road., Saint Helena CA 94574 – www.buehlervineyards.com – (707) 963–2155 – Hours: 10:00am – 4:00pm Appointment – Founded 1978, it is 20 minutes from the Silverado Trail to reach this isolated winery, but they make some good wines, that are reasonably priced. The tour is conducted by a family member and the whole experience is informative and relaxed. If you want something off the beaten path and want to stock your cellar this is the place for you. Map I

Buoncristiani Family Winery – At the Soda Canyon Caves – Bordeaux and Burgundy Blends – 2275 Soda Canyon Rd, Napa, CA 94558 – www.buonwine.com – (707) 259–1681 – Hours: 10am – 4:30pm Appointment – Wonderful wines poured in the lovely cafe tasting room inside this working cave. Map E3

Buhman Ranch – Wines: Bordeaux and Burgundy – 1331 Buhman Ave, Napa, CA 94558 – www.buhmanwines.com – (707) 227–7078 Hours: Appointment – This rustic cattle ranch in northern Carneros offers some nice wines in the vineyard. Map C

Burgess Cellars – New Location – Wines: Cabernet Sauvignon, Merlot, Syrah – 2921 Silverado Trail Napa CA 94558 - www.burgesscellars.com – (707) 963–4766 ?– Hours: Appointment – The 2020 Glass fire destroyed their buildings on the Deerpark slopes, so they bought the Luna facility on the southern Silverado Trail and opened there in July of 2021. It is much more convenient. Their Deerpark vineyards were first planted in the 1880's and Burgess started in 1972, when there were less than 30 wineries in Napa. They changed ownership right before the Glass fire. Map E3

Cade Winery – Beautiful Views on Howell Mountain – Wines: Cabernet blend, Sauvignon Blanc/Semillon. 360 Howell Mountain Road South Angwin CA 94508 – www.cadewinery.com – (707) 945–1220 – Hours: Appointment – This state of the art, LEEDS winery perched on the mountainside, enjoys spectacular valley views. The experience feels formal but the winery and caves are part of the tour. They are surprisingly more famous for the views and architecture than the wines. Map I

Cade13th Vineyard — Howell Mountain – Formerly the site of Ladera – Wines: Cabernet Sauvignon, Blends – 150 White Cottage Road South Angwin CA 94508 – www.cadewinery.com – (707) 965–2445 – Hours: Appointment – The original building was constructed in 1886 and transformed, rather than restored, by the new owners in 2000, by keeping the exterior stone walls and creating a new intra–structure to hold the winery equipment. It is an innovative approach. In 2018–19 the Plumpjack group purchased it and added their vineyards. Map I

Cain Vineyard and Winery – Spring Mountain – The 2020 Glass fire completely destroyed their buildings but the vineyards were spared. Check the website – Wines: Bordeaux - 3800 Langtry Road Saint Helena CA 94574 – www.cainfive.com – (707) 963–1616 Hours: Appointment – They are halfway up Spring Mountain Road, and along narrow Langtry Road. But they have great views and wonderful wines. They do limited tastings so plan well in advance. Map H

Cakebread Cellars – Popular Appointment Winery – Wines: Sauvignon Blanc, Chardonnay, Pinot Noir, Merlot, Syrah, Zinfandel, Cabernet Sauvignon, – 8300 Saint Helena Highway (Highway 29). Rutherford CA 94573 – www.cakebread.com – (800) 588–0298 – Hours: 10:00am – 4:00pm Appointment - This family winery, with the easy to remember name, did several expansions over the years to create a wonderful hospitality experience surrounded by vines on the broad valley floor. They offer numerous classes. They are located on the lines between the Rutherford and Oakville AVA's north of Mondavi. Navigation Tip: Going north on Highway 29 they are just past the Turnbull winery that looks very similar. Map F3

Calafia Cellars – Small – Wines: Bordeaux and Burgundy - 629 Fulton Lane Saint Helena CA 94574 – www.calafiacellars.com – (707) 963–0114 – Hours: 11:00am – 5:00pm – Hours: Appointment – The owner/winemaker has some serious winemaking chops, having honed his skills at Souverain, Mayacamas, Stag's Leap Vineyard and Hess Collection. They are small production of a red table wine in the Bordeaux style. Map G5

Caldwell Vineyards – Winery Caves in Coombsville – Wines: Bordeaux and Burgundy – 169 Kreuzer Lane Napa CA 94559 – www.caldwellvineyard.com – (707) 255–1294 – Hours: Appointment – Located in the hills to the east of the city of Napa. The winery is inside a thirty thousand square feet cave complex used by numerous labels. There are great views of the city of Napa in the distance. The ride down to the cave is on a steep gravel drive cut into the hillside so take your time. The vineyards you pass on the way sit above the caves. The tasting experience is fun, but for the enthusiast. Map D

Canard Vineyard – Calistoga – Wines: Bordeaux Blends – 1016 Dunaweal Lane Calistoga CA 94515 – www.canardvineyard.com – (707) 942–1149 – Hours: 10:30 am – 4:30pm by Appointment – Check for their tasting location since their previous, Fairwinds Estate, was destroyed in the 2020 Glass Fire that hit the north valley. Map Does not appear on map.

Cardinale Estate Wines – Serious Ultra-Premium Experience Wines: Cabernet Sauvignon blends – 7600 St Helena Highway (Highway 29). Oakville CA 94562 – www.cardinale.com – (707) 948–2643 – Hours: 10:30–5 Appointment – This long, stone building sits on a low hill on the east side of the road north of Yountville across from Far Niente. The tasting takes place in a classic conference room with the wine educator. They make great red wines with an exclusive feel. This is the old Pepi winery, now owned by the Jackson Family, the owner of Kendall Jackson. When you are standing in the parking lot look to the east, you will see the top of an extensive artificial cave complex which is a Jackson Family winery facility. Map F3

Carter Cellars – Calistoga – Wines: Bordeaux Blends – 1170 Tubbs Ln Calistoga, CA 94515 – www.cartercellars.com – (707)445–0311 Hours: 10:00am – 4:30pm Monday – Sunday Appointment – They share a space with Envy Wines. Map K

Castello di Amorosa – Northern Napa's Castle with Tours – Wines: Multiple from dry to sweet. 4045 North St Helena Highway (Highway 29). Calistoga 94515 – www.castellodiamorosa.com – (707) 967–6272 – Hours: 9am–6pm, 9am – 5pm November–February – People laughed when we called Napa Valley Disneyland for adults, and then this 12th century Tuscan–style castle/winery with 110 rooms, complete with dungeon, called "Castle of the Beloved" opened after 13 years of work. It has become one of Napa's most visited wineries and the tours are fun. Hint: You can rent the dungeon for Halloween. Now that is one party your friends will not forget! They offer guided and self–guided tours. Appointments required. Castles are cold in winter and cool in summer, so dress accordingly. Children are restricted to certain tours and there are too many stairs for babies and strollers. It is surrounded by vines, olive trees, chickens and the occasional sheep. Drive up and see the outside even if you do not plan to go in. They suffered damage in the 2020 Glass Fire. Map J

Cathiard Family Estate – Rutherford at the west end of Zinfandel Lane. 1978 – Red Blends – W. Zinfandel Lane St. Helena CA 94574 – (707) 302-5503 www.cathiardvineyard.com –This historic property, with its stone winery, was perviously Flora Springs. In 2020 it was sold to a French family. It is a lovely property with views. The vineyards are being converted to Biodynamic and a new winery was constructed. Map G2

Caves at Soda Canyon – Multiple Wineries – Wines: Bordeaux and Burgundy Blends – 2275 Soda Canyon Rd, Napa, CA 94558 www.the-cavesatsodacanyon.com – (707) 259–1681 – Hours: 10am 4:30pm Appointment – They are built into the top of the ridge overlooking the Stags Leap district, so expect a steep drive, but great views. The tasting takes place in the cave, and they feature the wines of the five partner wineries. Map E3

Caymus Vineyards – Famous Red – Navigation Tip: At the junction of Conn Creek, Skellenger and Rutherford Roads. Be early for your appointment. Wines: Cabernet Sauvignon, Zinfandel, Sauvignon Blanc, Chardonnay – 8700 Conn Creek Road Rutherford CA 94573 – www.caymus.com – (707) 967–3010 – Hours: 10:00am – 4:00pm – They are a premium winemaker with a great reputation and a favorite at restaurants. They do a seated tasting. Make sure you arrive early because they may give your spot away. In nice weather they do their tastings outside. They also have a tasting bar, and in wet weather they move into the barrel rooms, which are drafty, so bring a jacket. Navigation Tip: They are at the junction of Conn Creek, Skellenger and Rutherford Roads behind a foliage covered wall. Map F4

Ceja Vineyards – 22989 Burndale Road Sonoma, CA 95476 www.cejavineyards.com – (707) 255–3954 – Hours: 11am – 5pm – Their vineyards are in both Napa and Sonoma counties and their tasting room is accessible on Carneros Highway in Sonoma. Does not appear on map.

Celani Family Vineyards – Oak Knoll Collectors – Wines: Bordeaux and Burgundy – 2230 Big Ranch Road, Napa CA 94558 – www.celaniwines.com – (707) 255–5645 –Hours: Appointment - This private tasting for the Cabernet collector is in a Tuscan style home surrounded by vineyards, north of Trancas Street. . Map E2

Chappellet Winery and Vineyard – Sage Canyon Appointment Wines: Cabernet Sauvignon, Merlot, Cabernet Franc, Chardonnay, Chenin Blanc, Cuvee – 1581 Sage Canyon Road Saint Helena CA 94574 – www.chappellet.com – (707) 963–7136 – This is a world class, family run winery on the slopes of Pritchard Hill off Sage Canyon Road, east of the main valley. Started in 1967 they chose a perfect location for growing. These mountain roads are small and winding, so get directions. Allow twenty minutes from the Silverado Trail to their front door, which is at the near end of the winery buildings. Stay on the path to avoid the poison oak. Navigation Tip: On Sage Canyon Road there is a sign for Pritchard Hill on a mailbox that marks the turn. Driving east it is the third of three roads across from the parking lot by Hennessy Lake. As you go up the mountain take your time. After you go through a vineyard area with great views you will see small signs for the winery. Map F5

Charles Krug Winery – Great History – Wines: Cabernet Sauvignon, Merlot, Sauvignon Blanc, Chardonnay, Pinot Noir, Zinfandel, Cabernet Franc, Syrah – 2800 St Helena Highway North (Highway 29) Saint Helena CA 94574 – www.charleskrug.com (707) 967–2229 – Hours: 10:30am – 5:00pm Appointment. This is Napa's oldest operating winery, owned by Peter Mondavi's family. It was originally bought by the Mondavi family after WWII, but in the 1960's Robert Mondavi left and started his own eponymous winery. The impressive old winery building is where the tastings take place. They have an Italian style deli and coffee bar inside, so you can get food pairings with your wine. Tastings are done inside and out under the trees. The family owns some vineyards up and down the Napa Valley. Map G2

Charter Oak Winery – Tiny Downtown Saint Helena – Wines: Bordeaux, General French – 831 Charter Oak Ave, St Helena, CA 94574 www.charteroakwine.com – (707) 963–2298 – Hours: 10:00am – 4:30pm – Hours: Appointment – Art Gallery. This winery lives in the basement of a house, part of the tradition of home Italian winemakers who once filled the area. Map G5 Does not appear on map.

Chase Cellars - Saint Helena - Small and Charming with interesting wines - 2252 Sulphur Springs Ave, St Helena, CA 94574 - chasecellars.com - (707) 963-1284 - This family owned winery is located south of downtown Saint Helena on the revered Hayne Vineyard. They make Chardonnay, Zinfandel, Petite Sirah and a Cab Sauv. Map G2

Chateau Boswell – Premium – *Note: Rebuilding after the 2020 Glass fire.* – Wines: Chardonnay, Cabernet Sauvignon – 3468 Silverado Trail North Saint Helena CA 94574 – www.chateauboswellwinery.com – (707) 963-5405 – Hours: Appt. Located on the east side of the Silverado trail north of downtown Saint Helena. Their founding winemaker was the famous Andre Tchelistcheff, and their current is Phillipe Melka, so they aim for premium to ultra-premium. They source grapes from exceptional vineyards throughout California. Map J

Chateau Montelena Winery – Of the Judgment of Paris and Bottle Shock Fame – Wines: Chardonnay, Cabernet Sauvignon, Zinfandel, Riesling – 1429 Tubbs Lane Calistoga 94515 – www.montelena.com – (707) 942–5105 – Hours: 9:30 – 4:00pm Appointment – The winery was built into a hillside at the top of the valley in the late 1800's by the Tubbs family, as a gravity fed winery. It passed through another family that built the lake before the Barrett's began making wine there. They had only been at it a couple of years when their Chardonnay, a blend of Sonoma and Napa grapes, made a splash. It took the top score for a white wine against their American and French contemporaries at the 1976 Judgment of Paris blind tasting. Combined with the Stag's Leap Cellars win for their Cabernet, Napa suddenly became a serious player in the international wine world. They are located north of downtown Calistoga next to the Old Faithful Geyser. It is a gorgeous, classic building with remarkable grounds and a beautiful Asian style Jade Lake. The tasting room sits on top of the winery and the parking is below, so you pass the crush pad on the way up. This is fun during harvest when you will see the grape processing out front. There is a small parking lot on the upper level in case the walk up the two flights of stairs pose a problem. Map K

Checkerboard Vineyards – Calistoga Ultra–Premium for Collectors Wines: Bordeaux Blends – 4331 Azalea Springs Way, Calistoga – www.checkerboardvineyards.com – (707) 942–4112 – Appointments. Map K

Chiarello Family Vineyards – Downtown Inside Ottimo – Wines: An interesting variety – 6525 Washington St Yountville CA 94599 – www.chiarellovineyards.com – (707) 256–0750 – Hours: 10am–6pm Sunday 10am – 5pm – Celebrity chef Michael Chiarello's Ottimo store in Yountville has something for everyone, including his wines. Map E5

Chimney Rock Winery – Stags Leap's White Building – Wines: Cabernet Sauvignon, Fumé Blanc, Rosé of Cabernet Franc – 5350 Silverado Trail Napa CA 94558 – www.chimneyrock.com - 707) 257–2641 – Hours: 10:00am – 5:00pm Appointment - They are part of the Terlato Family Wineries who also owns Rutherford Hill Winery. They always do a good job of producing high quality wines and producing a satisfying tasting room experience. It is easy to spot from the Silverado Trail, a big white, South African Dutch–style building. The original owner lived in South Africa for many years. The name comes from the stone cliffs that tower over the vineyards. Map E3

Cliff Lede Vineyards – Charming Stags Leap District – Wines: Sauvignon Blanc, Cabernet Sauvignon, Claret – 1473 Yountville Cross Road Yountville CA 94599 – www.CliffLedeVineyards.com – (707) 944–8642 – Hours: 10:00am – 4:00pm Appointment – This is a charming winery on the northern edge of the Stags Leap district, just minutes from downtown Yountville. The staff is nice, the wines are excellent, the gardens and patio out back are gracious and relaxing. They have a small gift area. This is a nice place for a seated tasting with a group on a shady part of the patio. From the tasting room you can see the winery in the distance nestled against the hillside, connected to its caves. On the hillside above the winery is their associated Bed and Breakfast, the Poetry Inn. Map E3

Clos Du Val – Stags Leap District – Wines: Cabernet Sauvignon, Chardonnay, Merlot, Pinot Noir – 5330 Silverado Trail Napa CA 94558 – www.closduval.com – (707) 261–5200 – Hours: 10:00am – 5:00pm Appointment – This is a French–style winery, with good wines, a modern spacious tasting room, and extensive outdoor tasting areas. It was founded in 1972 by an American businessman and a French winemaker. They are known for their Bordeaux blends, but locally they are respected for their Pinot which they grow in the rolling hills of Los Carneros on the north side of Highway 121. Map E3

Clos Pegase Winery – Great Architecture – Wines: Chardonnay, Sauvignon Blanc, Pinot Noir, Merlot, Cabernet Sauvignon 1060 Dunaweal Lane Calistoga 94515 – (707) 942–4981 – www.clospegase.com Hours: 10:30–5:00pm – This is a dramatic building and the tasting room is tucked in the far–left corner. The building is a Michael Graves creation, although the signature colors were changed. Map K

Conn Creek Winery – Not Accepting Visitors - At the Crossroads – Wines: Cabernet Sauvignon, Cabernet Franc, Merlot – 8711 Silverado Trail South Saint Helena CA 94574 – www.conncreek.com – (707) 963–9100 – Hours: 10:00am – 4:00pm – This is a pleasant winery that is often missed because they are located at a busy intersection, but they make some good wines. When they first planted the vineyards, it was so rocky that they had to use explosives to break up some of the boulders. We are sure by now the sulfur taste is gone from the vines. They do a great wine blending seminar in a special room, where people can make a bottle to their taste. They remarkably assembled a startling array of barrels representing most of the sections of Napa. Being able to sample them side by side is a sure way to recognize how much location shapes flavors. Map G3

Continuum Estate – Wines: Cabernet Sauvignon, Cabernet Franc, Petit Verdot, Merlot – 1677 Sage Canyon Rd, St Helena, CA 94574 www.continuumestate.com – (707) 944–8100 – Hours: 10:00am – 4:00pm Appointment – This is an extraordinary estate on the top of the Vaca Mountains to the east of the valley with great views. This is the Tim Mondavi family winery. But it is not an easy appointment to arrange. Map F5

Corison Wines – Elegant Wines – Wines: Cabernet Sauvignon, Gewürztraminer – 987 St Helena Highway (Highway 29) Saint Helena CA 94574 – www.corison.com – (707) 963–0826 – Hours:

10:00am to 5:00pm Appointment – This is a conveniently located, small winery owned by the respected winemaker, Cathy Corison, who is known for her stellar Cabernets. The tasting is in the barrel room located inside of a pretty barn. The staff is knowledgeable and low key and the vineyards are right outside the back door. Map G2

Cosentino Winery – Not Accepting Visitors - Next to Mustard's Grill – Wines: Bordeaux, Burgundy, Gewürztraminer, Sangiovese, Dolcetto, Tempranillo, Viognier, Dessert – 7415 St Helena Highway (Highway 29) Yountville CA 94599 www.cosentinowinery.com – (707) 944–1220 – Hours: 10:00am – 5:00pm – This ivy–covered winery is just north of Yountville. It is a high energy tasting room next to Mustard's Grill. The wines are interesting and tasting and the staff is fun. They attract a younger crowd. Map E2

Covert Winery – Collectors in Coombsville – Wine: Bordeaux Style – 15 Chateau Lane, Napa CA 94558 www.covertestate.com – (707)337–5943 – Hours: Appointment. This cave winery with its very elegant tasting room inside the cave looks out over the rolling hills of Coombsville. Map D

Crocker and Starr – Saint Helena – Wines: Bordeaux Blends 700 Dowdell Ln, St Helena, CA 94574 – www.crockerstarr.com (707) 967–9111 – Hours: 10:00am to 3:00pm Appointment Charcuterie Artisanal Cheeses – This is an excellent winery down a road from Highway 29 by downtown Saint Helena. It is a partnership of a well known grower and respected woman winemaker and the experience is personal and interesting. Map G5

Crosby Roamann – Corporate Park in the Crusher District – Wines: Seriously good Bordeaux and Burgundy – 45 Enterprise Ct #6, Napa CA 94558 – www.crosbyroamann.com – (707) 266–6291 – Hours: Appointment. Map A1 Does not appear on map

Cuvaison Estate Carneros – Great Views – Wines: Pinot Noir, Cabernet Sauvignon, Chardonnay, Merlot, Syrah, Zinfandel, Port – 1221 Duhig Road Napa CA 94559 – www.cuvaison.com (707) 942–2455 Hours: 10:00am – 5:00pm Appointment – Their Carneros winery is across from Domaine Carneros. It is simple, elegant with spectacular views. Navigation Tip: Their driveway is directly across from the entrance to Domaine Carneros and the winery experiences could not be more different, considering the locations. Note: In 2021 they were starting a dramatic redo of their tasting building. Map C

Dakota Shy Winery – Collectors – Wines: Bordeaux and Burgundy – 771 Sage Canyon Road, Saint Helena – www.dakotashywine.com – (707) 244–1184 – Hours: Appt. Map F5

Darioush – A Persian Dream – Wines: Viognier, Cabernet Sauvignon, Shiraz, Chardonnay, Merlot, Pinot Noir – 4240 Silverado Trail

Napa CA 94558 – www.darioush.com – (707) 257–2345 - Hours: 10:30am – 5:00pm Appointment – Any Napa visitor from Persia must come to Darioush which is at the southern end of the Silverado Trail, south of the Stags Leap district. It is patterned after a Persian temple, with an elegant tasting bar, comfy stools and low seating around tables. The golden travertine was quarried in Iran, carved in Italy and assembled in Napa, on top of the caves. It is a family friendly place and always seems to attract the prettiest girls at the end of the day. Map E3

Darms Lane Wine – Family Winery – Wines: Cabernet Sauvignon, Petit Verdot, Chardonnay, Pinot Noir – 150 Darms Lane Napa, CA 94558 www.darmslanewine.com – (707) 224–4200 – Hours: Appointment – This is a charming family winery that makes good wines at a proper price in the south western part of the valley. The tasting is on their patio overlooking the vines and the valley beyond. Map E2

David Arthur Vineyards – Sage Canyon Appointment – Wines: Sauvignon Blanc, Chardonnay, Merlot, Cabernet Sauvignon – 1521 Sage Canyon Road Saint Helena CA 94574 – www.davidarthur.com – (707) 963–5190 – Hours: Appointment – This is a respected producer perched on a ridge overlooking the Valley. It is one of the wineries tucked up in the hills of Sage Canyon. The tasting is relaxed, but plan well in advance. Map F5

David Fulton Winery – Wine: General French – 825 Fulton Lane, Saint Helena CA 94574 – www.davidfultonwinery.com – (707) 967–0719 – Hours: Appointment – This is tiny winery in downtown Saint Helena that goes back to the earliest wine making in the area. Map G5. Does not appear on map

Davies Vineyards – Downtown Saint Helena, Related to Schramsberg – Wines: Bordeaux and Burgundy – 1210 Grayson Ave, St Helena CA 94574 – www.daviesvineyards.com – (707) 963–5555 – Hours: 9:45am – 5:00pm Appointment – Seated Tasting, Pairings – This is a downtown winery and tasting room for the family that makes the Schramsberg sparkling wines. It is in a modern stone building in downtown Saint Helena. Map G5

Davis Estates – Calistoga Silverado Trail – 4060 Silverado Trail, Calistoga CA 94515 – www.davisestates.com – (707) 942–0700 Hours: 10:00am – 4:00pm Appointment – Food Pairings – This little winery property was once part of the Larkmead property that belonged to the family of Lillie Coit in the 1800's. It went through several owners who each worked on developing the winery, because the property is not large enough for many vines. Finally, the Davis family brought it to completion and they source excellent grapes. It is a lovely property with nice views of the valley. Do not confuse them with the Davis Family Winery of Healdsburg, or the Davies Family, the still wine label of the makers of Schramsberg. Map J

Del Dotto Vineyards (Atlas Peak) – Historic Caves – Wines: Cabernet Sauvignon, Cabernet Franc, Merlot, Pinot Noir, Sangiovese, Zinfandel, Port – 1055 Atlas Peak Road Napa CA 94558 www.DelDottoVineyards.com – (707) 256–3332 – Hours: 11:00am – 5:00pm Appointment – This is their original Napa property. These caves on Atlas Peak Road are some of the oldest in Napa, built by the architect of Inglenook and Greystone. The Del Dotto team takes a hands-on approach and tastings are normally done as part of a tour. They love to show how various barrels influence the flavors of the wine. Both wineries, old and new, are remarkable in their own ways. The wines are popular, the tour is a lot of fun and they draw plenty of repeat visitors. They are known to pour big tastings, so either hire a driver, or have a designated driver. The interior is elaborate funk. Map E1

Del Dotto Estate Winery and Caves (Zinfandel Lane) Wines: Cabernet Sauvignon, Cabernet Franc, Merlot, Pinot Noir, Sangiovese, Zinfandel, Port. 1445 St Helena Highway (Highway 29) Saint Helena CA 94574 – www.DelDottoVineyards.com – (707) 256–3332 – Hours: 11:00am – 5:00pm Appointment – This is their second winey near the intersection of Zinfandel Lane and Highway 29; look for the two large amphorae outside the gates. The winery is mostly underground and remarkable in an explosion of Italian marble. You walk downstairs to enter. The best experience is as part of the cave tour. Map F3

Piazza Del Dotto – Property Number Three – Wines: Cabernet Sauvignon, Cabernet Franc, Merlot, Pinot Noir, Sangiovese, Zinfandel, Port – 7466 St. Helena Highway (Highway 29) Napa, CA 94558 – www.DelDottoVineyards.com – 707-963-2134 Hours: 11:00am – 5:00pm Appointment – This is the most ambitious Del Dotto winery yet, with an expansive hospitality building with tasting bars and outdoor seating areas, extensive cave and other entertainments. It is just north of downtown Yountville. Map E2

Diamond Creek Vineyards - Diamond Mountain – Cabernet Blends for Collectors – www.diamondcreekvineyards.com – (707) 942-6926 – 1500 Diamond Mountain Rd, Calistoga, CA 94515 – This is a long-time premium grower on Diamond Mountain just south of Calistoga. Many years ago, they almost scandalized Napa by being the first winery to charge $100 for a bottle of wine. The prices of course have not come down. The property is a short way up the mountain and each vineyard is quite distinctive. In recent years it changed hands from the original owners. Visits often include a tour of the property, and the private tastings are done in an expansive, elegant room, with views of the very pretty vineyards. Map K

Diamond Mountain Vineyard – At the Top – Formerly Constant Diamond– Wines: Cabernet Franc, Merlot, Cabernet Sauvignon – 2121 Diamond Mountain Road Calistoga CA 94515 – www.diamondmountainvineyard.com – (707) 942–0707 – This is a premium winery located at the top the mountain. The road is long, narrow and steep. They enjoy spectacular views and the tasting is special. MapK

Domaine Carneros – Elegant Sparkling Wines in Southern Napa – Wines: Brut Cuvee, Brut Rosé, Le Reve Blanc de Blancs, Pinot Noir. Wines can be ordered by the glass – 1240 Duhig Road Napa 94559 www.domainecarneros.com – (707) 257–0101 – Hours: 10:00am – 6:00pm Appointment – This chateau towers over Carneros like a birthday cake with candles alight. You cannot ignore it, and you should not because it offers one of Napa's most romantic sparkling wine experiences. The building is modeled on the Taittinger family's French chateau, with large patios and gorgeous tasting rooms. The building sits high because the winery is underneath, and they offer tours into the depths that explain the sparkling wine 'methode champenoise'. Out in back is a second winery make non–sparkling Pinot Noir, which with Chardonnay are the main grapes used for Champagne. The sit–down tasting is either outside with the great views, or inside a tasting room reminiscent of Versailles. Wines are offered by the glass and flight, which should be shared. Sparkling wines are so light and fresh they often disguise the significant amount of alcohol they contain. Map D

Domaine Chandon – Wines: Sparkling and Still wines –
1 California Dr. Yountville 94599 – www.domainechandon.com – (707) 944–2280 – Hours: 10:00am – 5:00pm – This is by downtown Yountville, with beautiful grounds, a large tasting bar, seating areas, snacks and side dishes. Domaine Chandon was the first European owned Champagne Company to invest here in the 1970's. It is not an intimate experience. At the end of the day it turns into a bit of a party. Between its history, reputation, hospitality, tours, and great wines they continue to be one of Napa's most visited locations. Map E4

DR Stephens Estate – Collectors in a Northern Napa Cave– Wines: Cabernet Sauvignon, Chardonnay, Pinot Noir, Sauvignon Blanc – 3520 Silverado Trail North Napa, CA 94558 – www.drstephensestate.com Phone: (707) 963–2908. Map J Does not appear on map. They also make a second lable called **Collateral**.

Duckhorn Vineyards – A Nice Seated Tasting – Wines: Sauvignon Blanc, Merlot, Cabernet Sauvignon – 3027 Silverado Trail North Saint Helena CA 94574 – www.duckhorn.com – (707) 967–2000 – Hours: 10:00am – 4:00pm Appointment – Their beautiful craftsman–style mansion at the corner of Lodi Lane and the Silverado Trail is a great landmark. This is the narrowest part of the valley, and across from the vineyards, the stone cliffs tower above the road. They do a wonderfully relaxed, seated tasting, either in the sunny salon or out on the patios. They have a great collection of duck decoys and sculptures. The grounds are lovely with a view of the vineyards. It makes a real statement, you are in the heart of wine country. Map J

Ehlers Estate – Small, Beautiful, Biodynamic Winery – Wines: Cabernet Sauvignon, Merlot, Sauvignon Blanc, Cabernet Franc, Zinfandel 3222 Ehlers Lane Saint Helena CA 94574 – www.ehlersestate.com (707) 963–5972 – Hours: 10:00am – 4:00pm This is a beautiful, small winery located in a great old stone barn, with an interesting tasting room. Just behind it, and visible through the windows, is the winery. Alongside it is a large shaded garden with tables and bocce courts. They have a nice staff. The wines are Biodynamic. Map J

Eleven Eleven – Trancas Street Convenient – Wines: Bordeaux and Burgundy, General French – 620 Trancas Street, Napa CA 94558 – www.elevenelevenwines.com – (707) 224–2211 – Hours: 10:00am – 4:00pm Appointment – They are at north edge of the city of Napa. They produce wonderful wines that they pour in an elegant space that blends from inside to out. The facility that also serves custom crush clients. They are very convenient to downtown Napa. Map E2

Elizabeth Spencer Wines – Tasting Room in Rutherford – Wines: Sauvignon Blanc, Chardonnay, Pinot Noir, Syrah, Cabernet Sauvignon – 1165 Rutherford Road Rutherford CA 94573 www.elizabethspencerwines.com – (707) 963–6067 – Hours: 10:00am – 6:00pm – The original Rutherford Post Office from 1872, across from BV. Recently purchased by Boisset, who makes things fun, and it now is home to a collection of culinary exhibits. Map F3

Ellman Family – Collectors with a downtown tasting salon- Wines: Cabernet Sauvignon – 1461 First Street, Napa CA 94558– www.ellmanfamilyvineyards.com – (707) 947–3010 – Hours: Appointment – Vineyards are near Reynolds. Map E3

Elyse Winery – Small & South of Yountville – Wines: Zinfandel, Cabernet Sauvignon, Petite Syrah, Syrah, Rhone Blends – 2100 Hoffman Lane Napa CA 94573 – www.elysewinery.com – (707) 944–2900 – Hours: 10:00am – 5:00pm Appointment. Map E2

Envy Wines – Near the Calistoga Geyser – Wines: Cabernet Sauvignon, Petite Syrah, Sauvignon Blanc – 1170 Tubbs Lane Calistoga CA 94515 www.envywine.com – (707) 942–4670 – Hours: 10:00am – 4:30pm Appointment – They are located down a curving drive just off Tubbs lane to the north of downtown Calistoga. They are relaxed and friendly with good wines. It is a pretty building in a convenient northern location. Map K

Etude – Carneros Pinot – Wines: Pinot Noir, Merlot, Cabernet Sauvignon, Pinot Blanc, Pinot Gris – 1250 Cuttings Wharf Road Napa CA 94559 – www.etudewines.com – (707) 257–5300 – Hours: 10:00am – 4:30pm Appointment – This is a larger facility with interesting buildings and a European feel. They have been producing high quality Pinot Noir for many years and continue to do so. wines. Map D

Failla – Great Pinots North of Saint Helena – Wines: Pinot Noir, Viognier, Syrah, Chardonnay – 3530 Silverado Trail, Saint Helena CA 94574 – www.faillawines.com – (707) 963–0530 – Hours: 10:00am – 5:00pm Appointment – They make some of the best Pinot Noir in Napa because the grapes come from Sonoma's Coastal region, which has ideal conditions for that finicky grape. They have cool caves with the entire winery inside. They have a good staff that works both in a charming bungalow tasting room, and in the cave tasting. It is a seated tasting and you will be part of a small group. They are across the street from the Rombauer entrance, which is good to know since the Failla sign is not obvious, being small, and written on the mailbox. Map J

Fairchild – Ultra Premium for Collectors – Wines: Cabernet Sauvignon – P.O. Box 2000, Saint Helena CA 94574 – www.fairchildwines.com – (707) 963–9990 – Hours: Appointment – members@ fairchildwines.com – Their tastings are at a home in the Deer Park section on the slopes of Howell Mountain. These are serious wines that the owner pours for you. Map I Does not appear on map

Fairwinds Estate – Calistoga on the Silverado Trail – Note: Their tasting room and winery were destroyed in the 2020 Glass fire, wine club members can taste in the cave by appt. Map K

Fantesca Estate – Spring Mountain Collectors – Cabernet Blends – 2920 Spring Mountain Rd, St Helena, CA – www.fantesca.com – (707) 968-9229 – They are tucked a short way up Spring Mountain Road at the end of a long driveway. The winemaker is Heidi Barrett and it is owned by the founders of Best Buy. They have a home on the other side of the rise which can be reached through the straight through wine cave next to the simple winery. The views from the crush pad of the vineyards and the valley below are nice and the wines are first class. The tasting is in a conference room above the winery and the fees are a bit high, considering the low-key experience. Map H

Falcor Winery – Corporate Park– Wines: Bordeaux Blends – 2511 Napa Corporate Drive, Napa CA 94558 –www.falcorwines.com – (707) 255–6070 – Hours: Appointments. Map A1 Not on map

Far Niente – A Great Estate – Wines: Cabernet Sauvignon, Chardonnay, Dolce, Sauterne style – 1350 Acacia Dr. Oakville CA 94558 – www.farniente.com – (707) 944–2861 – Hours: 10:00am – 4:00pm Monday–Saturday Appointment – This is an architectural jewel surrounded by wonderful grounds, ponds, fountains, cork oaks and event spaces. The tasting can include a tour of the winery and the car collection. They make wonderful world–class wines and do a sit–down tasting inside and in the gardens. When making your appointment take special care to determine which experience you want to do. If you love architecture make sure you do the tour. Map F3

Farella Vineyards – Coombsville – Relaxed Family Winery Wines: Sauvignon Blanc, Merlot, Cabernet Blanc, Blends – 2222 North Third Ave. Napa CA 94558 – www.farella.com – (707) 254–9489 – Hours: Appointment – This charming winery sits in the hills on the beautiful east side of Napa. The property is in its second generation and their knowledge of their vineyards shows in their wonderful wines. The tasting is relaxed, at home Napa, and on a completely different level from the 'stand at the bar' tasting most people are accustomed to. They vineyards were planted in 1977 by the father, Frank Farella, and they were the first Coombsville winery to produce a Cabernet Sauvignon. Son Tom Farella, the longtime wine maker. They were the authors of the petition to have Coombsville made an official American Viticulture Area, or AVA. Map D

Faust – Perched on a Hill in St. Helena – Wines: Cabernet and other Bordeaux vareitals – 2867 St Helena Hwy, St Helena, CA 94574 – www.faustwines.com – (707) 200-2560 – Hours: Appointment – The main building was constructed in the late 1800's. Today it is connected with Quintessa and Russian River's Flowers, to feature Cabernet blends that come from their vineyard in Coombsville, a relatively cool AVA to the east of downtown Napa. The renovation turned it into a lovely, comfortable experience, with views of the valley and plenty of places to be sit. They are perched on a small hill just north of Beringer, and the building is painted a dark brown that makes it blend. There is a small winery facility onsite. Map G2

Favia Winegrowers – Coombsville Collectors – Wines: Bordeaux and Burgundy – P.O. Box 6978, Napa CA 94558 – www.faviawine.com – (707) 256–0875 – Hours: Appt. Map D

Fe Wines - Spring Mountain - Two Cabernet Blends - Saint Helena - www.fewines.com - 707-244-1191 - This is a newer winery with a small organic vineyard on the lower slopes of Spring Mountain, bordered by Bothe Park. The land was not previously farmed and the first grapes were harvested in 2016. They were made into the estate wines starting in 2018 by winemaker Aaron Potts, a local and respected consultant. They make two big pricey red blends. The property is rustic and charming and the name Fe comes from the scientific notation for Iron because the soil is high in that rugged mineral. Map H Does not appear on map

Fleury Winery – Unique – Wines: Bordeaux varietals – 950 Galleron Road, Rutherford CA 94574 – www.fleurywinery.com (707) 967–8333 – Hours: Appointment – This is a fun, high energy tasting room but watch out for large pours! Map G2

Flora Springs Winery – Tasting room – Wines: Cabernet Sauvignon, Sangiovese, Merlot, Rosato, Chardonnay, Pinot Grigio, Blends – 677 South St Helena Highway (Highway 29). Saint Helena CA 94574 – www.florasprings.com (866) 967–8032 Hours: 10:00am – 5:00pm

Their Highway 29 tasting room is a modern, architecturally interesting place. It includes a reserve tasting room and two outdoor seating areas. It is across the street from V. Sattui next to a large market. Map F3

Foley Johnson– Rutherford Variety – 8350 St Helena Highway (Hwy 29). Rutherford CA 94573 – www.foleyjohnsonwines.com (707) 963–1980 – Hours: 10:00am – 5:00pm Appointment This is part of the Foley Family Wine Group which owns an impressive portfolio of small, premium wineries. This winery is used as a sort of ambassador for the wine club that incorporates many of the labels. Map F3

Fontanella Family Winery – Mount Veeder Family Winery – Wines: Chardonnay, Cabernet Sauvignon and Zinfandel – 1721 Partrick Road Napa CA 94558 – www.fontanellawinery.com – (707) 252–1017 – Hours: Appointment – A friendly family winery a bit of a ride up Mount Veeder, it comes with great views. They are a charming couple with years of experience, and they produce solid wines with lots of character. Map B

Forman Vineyards – Small and Ultra–Premium – Wines: Cabernet Blend, Chardonnay. 1501 Big Rock Road Saint Helena CA 94574 – www.formanvineyard.net – (707) 963–3900 – Hours: Appointment – They are in a canyon, down a steep road and they make wonderful wines. Ric Forman was Sterling's founding winemakerl. Be on the lookout for signs as they are minimal. Map I

Forthright Winery – Small for Collectors – Wines: Bordeaux & Burgundy – 2255 Dry Creek Road Napa, CA, 94558 Appointment – www. forthrightwinery.com – A small winery that sources grapes from their own small vineyard and others. Map B

Fortunati Vineyards – A small family winery with good wines at reasonable prices – Wines: Bordeaux and Burgundy – 980 Salvador Ave, Napa, CA 94558 – www.fortunativineyards.com - (707) 255–9300 – Hours: 10:00am – 5:00pm Appointment – They are located just outside the city of Napa, but convenient from the downtown. The wines are nicely priced. Map E2

Frank Family Vineyards – Gracious and Fun Calistoga – Wines: Chardonnay, Sparkling, Cabernet Sauvignon, Zinfandel, Sangiovese 1091 Larkmead Lane Calistoga CA 94574 – www.frankfamilyvineyards.com – (707) 942–0859 – Hours: 10:00am – 5:00pm Appointment – The tasting is in a beautiful craftsman style mansion, with spacious rooms and surrounded by beautiful grounds. They are well–known for their humor and style. This is the site of the historic Larkmead Winery. They have a nice picnic area, and first–rate wines including a delicious sparkling wine in the rich and creamy Grand Cru style. Map J

Freemark Abbey – Great Traditions – Wines: Chardonnay, Viognier, Merlot, Cabernet Sauvignon, Sauvignon Blanc, Zinfandel, Zinfandel Port, Petit Syrah, and Syrah – 3022 St Helena Highway (Highway 29) at Lodi Lane, Saint Helena CA 94574 – www.freemarkabbey.com – (800) 963–9694 – Hours: 10:00am – 5:00pm Appointment – The site first became a winery in 1886. The main building dates to 1899 when it was the Lombarda Cellars. They shipped a great deal of wine to the Italian stone masons in Barre, Vermont, the site of America's largest marble and granite quarries. It has passed through numerous owners and since 1966 has been owned by a group of families. They produce a wide variety of well–made wines. This is a charming winery with a nice outdoor patio and lots of seating plus a tasting bar. Freemark Abbey is a combination of the partner's last names. Map J

Frias Family – In the City of Napa – Wines: Bordeaux and Burgundy – 1886 El Centro Ave, Napa 94558 – www.friasfamilyvineyard.com – (707)–927–5106 – Hours: 10 – 3 Monday–Sunday Appointment. Map H Does not appear on map

Frisinger Winery – Collectors Mount Veeder – Wines: Bordeaux and Burgundy – 3033 Dry Creek Rd, Napa, CA 94558 – www.frisingerfamilywine.com – (707) 338–5009 – Hours: Appointment – This family has been selling their grapes to other wineries for years, before returning to their original idea of making their own wines. So, the wines have a good history and an authentic story. Map B

Frog's Leap Winery – Remarkable Organic Winery – Wines: Merlot, Zinfandel, Chardonnay, Sauvignon Blanc, Cabernet Sauvignon, Syrah, Blends – 8815 Conn Creek Road Rutherford CA 94558 – www.frogsleap.com – (800) 959–4704 – Hours: 10:00am – 4:00pm Appointment – This organic winery has a beautiful green hospitality center. They also taste on the patios, the garden and in the historic red barn. They make great wines; have a wonderful tour and a lovely staff. They have been organic growers for many years. The signs on the street are not big, so watch the numbers and look for the BIG red barn on the north side of the road. The tasting room is to the right. Map F4

Futo Estate – Western Oakville Hillsides – Big Cabernet Blends for Collectors – 1575 Oakville Grade, Oakville, CA 94562 – www.futoestate.com – (707) 944-9333 – This rather extraordinary winery is perched on a hill in the very pricey west side of Oakville. Coming from Hwy 29 it is accessed by the first road to the left past the Far Niente driveway. They are located between Promontory and Bond, and the wines are on the same elevated level, so the wines are expensive. Map F3

Gamble Family Vineyards – Ultra–Premium for Collectors – Wines: Bordeaux, Burgundy Blends – 7554 Saint Helena Highway, Yountville CA 94559 – www.gamblefamilyvineyards.com (707) 944–2999 – The hospitality space is just off Highway 29 near Cardinale. The buildings are spare, white farm architecture and the focus is the wines, not the place or the architecture. The vineyards, which are in sight, extend all the way east to the Silverado Trail. These are big, impressive wines. Map F3

Gandona Estate – Ultra–Premium Mountain Vineyards - Wines: Bordeaux Blends 1533 Sage Canyon Rd, St Helena, CA 94574 – www.gandona.com – (707) 967-5550 . Map F5

Gargiulo Vineyards – Oakville Charm for Collectors - Wines: Bordeaux Blends – 575 Oakville Cross Rd Napa CA 94558 – www.gargiulovineyards.com – (707) 944–2770 – Hours: 10:30am – 3:30pm Appointment – This is a charming private winery with great views of Napa's best vineyards. They spent three years re–engineering their land before planting their grapes. The Gargiulo family has a long tradition with agriculture, and they know how to make a great bottle of wine. They do a relaxed, elegant seated tasting at specific times with a knowledgeable staff. They are surrounded by some of Napa's most prestigious wineries; Silver Oak, Rudd, Groth, Vine Cliff, Harlan, Cardinale and Far Niente. Map F4

Gemstone – Collectors – just north of the Yountville Cross Road on the Silverado Trail – Wines: Bordeaux and Burgundy Blends P.O. Box 3477, Yountville CA 94559 – www.gemstonewine.com – (707) 944–0944 – This is a simple tasting in a home, with a space to host guests and vineyards outside. Map E3

Ghost Block – Oakville, Part of the Napa Wine Company – Bordeaux and Burgundy, General French – 7830–40 Highway 29, Oakville CA – www.ghostblockwine.com – (707) 944–1710 Hours:10:00am – 3:30pm Appointment – the Perlissa family has been farming Napa for over a hundred years. Their family, the Hoxseys, run the Napa Wine Company which is an important custom crush facility. They converted their group tasting room into a private tasting room for their Ghost Block Wines and their other family labels. Map F3

Girard Winery – Calistoga – 1077 Dunaweal Lane, Calistoga, CA 94515 – Wines: Cabernet Sauvignon, Cabernet Franc, Petite Syrah, Zinfandel, Chardonnay, Sauvignon Blanc www.girardwinery.com – 707–234–4151 – Hours: 10:00am – 5:00pm Appointment – This is a well-respected label that is now owned by a group that manages numerous wineries. The Calistoga property is the winery facility and it features a spacious tasting area that looks out at the vines. Map K

Godspeed Vineyards – Mount Veeder Fruit – Chardonnay, Cabernet Sauvignon, Malbec, Blends – 3655 Mt. Veeder Road Napa Ca 94559 707–254–7766 – Hours: Appointment – A small estate winery producing three reasonably priced wines. Navigation Tip: Take the Oakville Grade to Mount Veeder Road, then south to the vineyards. Do not go north from Redwood Road. Not shown on our maps.

Goosecross Cellars – Yountville Charm – Wines: Bordeaux and Burgundy – 1119 State Lane Yountville CA 94599 – www.goosecross.com – (707) 944–1986 – Hours: 10:00am – 4:30pm Appointment – This small winery went through a major transformation to create a new facility and tasting room with outdoor patio tasting areas and great views. The wine list and the staff are wonderful. Near downtown Yountville. Map E3

Green and Red – A Unique Experience in Eastern Napa – 3208 Chiles Pope Valley Road Saint Helena, CA 94574 – www.greenandred.com (707)–965–2346 – Hours: Appointment – This second generation winery is for the adventurous, in Chiles Valley. The family started farming their hillside vineyards in the 1970's and have sold their grapes to excellent wineries. Their own wines are reasonably priced, and the story is wonderful. The name comes from the red chert and green serpentine in the soil of their vineyards. Map F5

Grgich Hills Cellar – Judgment of Paris Wine Maker – Wines: Chardonnay, Fumé Blanc, Violetta, Cabernet Sauvignon, Zinfandel, Merlot 1829 St Helena Highway South(Highway 29) Rutherford CA – www.grgich.com – (707) 963–2784 – Hours: 9:30am – 4:30pm – Tours – Grgich Hills has a great reputation and what they lack in 'pretty', they make up for with friendly, quality and value. The windowless tasting room was recently the barrel room. Mike Grgich (Pronounced 'gur gitch'), from Croatia, worked with Beaulieu Vineyard's revered winemaker Andre Tchelistcheff. Later he was the winemaker at Chateau Montelena when they produced their top ranked Chardonnay at the 1976 Judgment of Paris that put Napa on the wine map. Grgich Hills Winery (named for the Hills Bros. coffee family that is the other partner) was born on July 4th. 1977. They have Biodynamic vineyards that are managed by Mike's nephew and the winery is managed by his daughter. The tasting room staff is knowledgeable and relaxed. This is a Wine Train stop. In 2023 Mike turned one hundred years old! Map F3

Groth Vineyards – Big Pink – Wines: Cabernet Sauvignon, Chardonnay, Sauvignon Blanc – 750 Oakville Cross Road Oakville CA 94562 – www.grothvineyards.com – (707) 754–4254 – Hours: 10:00am – 4:00pm Appointment – This is a grand building in pink stucco with good wines and a beautiful tasting space. This is quintessential Oakville, so they range from Premium to Ultra-Premium. Map F3

Haber Family – Collectors – Wines: Bordeaux and Burgundy 345 Pine Breeze Drive Angwin CA 94508 –www.haberfamilyvineyards.com – (707) 965–9177 – Hours: Appointment - A small Howell Mountain family winery. Does not appear on map

Hagafen Cellars – Oak Knoll Kosher Wines – Wines: Riesling, Syrah, Cabernet Franc – 4160 Silverado Trail Napa CA 94558 –

www.hagafen.com – (707) 252–0781 – Hours: 10:00am – 5:00pm – Technically Oak Knoll AVA is across the road, but they share the qualities of this unique area. This is a nice, open air tasting room with kosher wines that have been served at the White House. The owner was one of Domaine Chandon's first employees. He has run Hagafen Cellars, which is the Hebrew word for wine, for many years for a devoted clientele. Map E3

Hall Wines – Wine and Sculpture – Wines: Cabernet Sauvignon, Merlot, Sauvignon Blanc – 401 St Helena Highway South (Hwy 29). Saint Helena CA 94574 – They have a second location off Rutherford Road called the Katherine Hall winery that can visited by Appointment – www.hallwines.com – (707) 967–2626 – Hours: 10:00am – 5:30pm. This larger winery is across from Louis M Martini, and it is a modern Architectural design that doubles as an exhibition space for the owner's art collection, including the giant bunny at the front of the property leaping through the vines, that you cannot miss. The floor to ceiling windows in the main tasting room are cool. They make good wines and have a pleasant staff. For the enthusiast, visit their beautiful mountain top Katherine Hall winery caves. This is a more expensive visit, but the views are great, and the sit–down tasting is in one Napa's most beautiful caves. It is lined with antique bricks from Austria and the hallways feature smaller pieces from their sculpture collection. Map G2

Hans Fahden Vineyards – Mountain Location. This winery is most popular as an event space. – Wines: Cabernet Sauvignon 4855 Petrified Forest Rd Calistoga CA 94515 – www.hansfahden.com – (707) 942–6760 – Hours: Appointment. Map K

Harlan Estate – High End Collector Trophy Wines – Cabernet Blends – www.HarlanEstate.com – At a $1000.00 a bottle by allocation they don't need to be in the directory, but people ask where they are located so…! Their other label Bond is located nearby. Map F3

HdV - Hyde de Villaine Wines – Trancas Street Convenient – Wines: Chardonnay, Pinot Noir, Syrah, Cabernet Blend – 588 Trancas Street, Napa 94558 – www.hdvwines.com – (707) 251-9121– Hours 10:am – 5:00pm Appointment – This little winery on Trancas Street is a partnership of two families connected by marriage. Their central themes are Pinot and Chardonnay. The vines are in Los Carneros and on Sonoma Mountain. Map E3

Heitz Wine Cellars – Well Respected Label – Wines: Cabernet Sauvignon, Chardonnay, Grignolino, Rosé, Zinfandel, Port 436 St Helena Highway (Highway 29). South Saint Helena CA 94574 – www.heitzcellar.com – (707) 963–3542 – Hours: 11:00am – 4:30pm Appointment – This recently redone tasting room is conveniently located just south of downtown Saint Helena. Heitz is one of Napa's most respected names. Their wines have a great history, and the vineyards and home ranch where they also host guests are in a canyon off the Silverado Trail next to the Joseph Phelps winery. The tasting room is on the site of the original winery. It changed hands and the new owners performed a complete transformation of the site. Map G2

Hendry Wines – Mount Veeder – Wines: Albariño, Pinot Gris, Chardonnay, Rosé, Pinot Noir, Primitivo, Blends, Zinfandel, Cabernet Sauvignon – 3104 Redwood Road Napa CA 94558 – www.hendry-wines.com – (707) 226–8320 – Hours: Appointment with Tour – The property has been in the family since the 1930's and there have been vineyards there since the 1860's. They do a great tour of the vineyards. You should plan on spending two hours. It is in an area with only a few other wineries. Navigation Tip: It is 2.5 miles from Highway 29 on the way to the Hess Collection. Map B

Hess Persson Estates – Art Collection on Mount Veeder – Wines: A wide variety, Olive Oil, Vinegar – 4411 Redwood Road Napa 94558 – www.hesspersssonestates.com – (707) 255–1144 – Hours: 10:00am – 5:30pm – This destination winery houses a world class modern art collection on several floors of an historic stone barn, facing another barn that houses a state–of–the–art winery. The tasting room and gift shop are worth seeing by themselves. The barns are classic historic Napa and owned by the Christian Brothers Winery who have their center next door. Hess is located on Mount Veeder in the southwest corner of Napa, north of Carneros. The ride there on Redwood road is winding. The outstanding art collection makes the ride very much worth the effort. Map B

Hestan Vineyards – Downtown Yountville with Cookware
Wines: Bordeaux and Burgundy – 6548 Washington Street Yountville CA 94559 – www.hestanvineyards.com – (707) 945–1002 – Hours: 11:00am – 6:00pm – This tasting room doubles as a showroom for this family's well known cookware. Map B

Hill Family Estate – Downtown Tasting Room – Wines: Chardonnay, Pinot Noir, Merlot, Cabernet Sauvignon, Syrah – 6512 Washington Street, Yountville CA 94599 – www.hillfamilyestate.com – (707) 944–9580 – Hours: 10:00am – 6:00pm – Their tasting room is in the center of Yountville, but do not let the location hide the fact that this is a winery with a great deal of depth. They own numerous vineyards around Napa and have been selling grapes to top wineries for many years. Besides the fun tasting in town, they also host tastings at a nearby property on Solano Ave. These are wonderful, authentic folks. Map E5

Holman Cellars – Corporate Park – 918 Enterprise Way G, Napa, CA 94558 – www.holmancellars.com – (707) 287–7557 Hours: Appt. Map A1 Does not appear on map

Honig Cellars – Charming Outside Tasting – Wines: Sauvignon Blanc, Cabernet Sauvignon – 850 Rutherford Road Rutherford CA 94573 www.honigcellars.com – (707) 963–5618 – Hours: 10:00am – 4:00pm Appointment – Their tasting patio is relaxed and stylish, and the mood is entertaining and gracious. They also do a more private, reserve tasting inside at a conference table. It is a serious look at their library wines, and it gives you a chance to realize that they own some very good vineyards in Rutherford. This is a family business in their third generation and the younger generation still brings a lot of enthusiasm to the game. Map F4

Hoopes Vineyards – Coombsville – Wines: Bordeaux and Burgundy 6204 Washington Street, Yountville CA 94559 – www.hoopesvineyard.com – (707) 944–1869 – Appt. Map D

Hope and Grace Winery - Downtown Yountville - Interesting Single Varietal wines including Bordeaux and Burgundy styles, including Malbec, Lagrein, Petite Verdot - 6540 Washington Street, Yountville, California, 94559 - www.hopeandgracewines.com - (707)-944-2500 - This was one of Yountville's first tasting rooms and longevity speaks volumes about the quality of the wines and the unique selection that they offer. The charming space sits in the middle of the shopping area and it is well worth the visit. The winemaker has a long history in this area and that is obvious in where they source their fruit. Map E5

Hourglass – Calistoga Collectors – Wines: Bordeaux and Burgundy – 4208 Silverado Trail N, Calistoga, CA 94515 – www.hourglasswines.com – (707) 968–9332 – Hours: 10:00am – 4:00 pm Appointment – This is a beautiful little cave winery on the east side of the Silverado Trail in the north part of the valley. The wines are priced for collectors. Map J

Hudson Vineyards – Wines: Bordeaux and Burgundy Blends 5398 Carneros Highway, Napa CA 94558 – www.hudsonvineyards.com – (707)–255–1455 – Hours: Appointment – This is a remarkable estate winery owned by long time growers on the north side of the Carneros Highway. They make a wonderful variety of wines that go beyond the supposed limits of this cool region. Look for the five flag poles. When bud break appears, or harvest begins, they run up the Jolly Roger, to show that they are an independent, and not a corporate property like many of their Carneros neighbors. Map C

Hunter Glenn Estate – Multi-Generation Family Winery South of Yountville – Wines: Bordeaux and Burgundy Blends – www.hunterglenn.com – Hours: Appointment – Caroline@hunterglenn.com – The brother and sister team that grow the grapes, make the wine and market it bottle by bottle are the fourth generation on the lovely vineyards, tucked against the Mayacamas mountains. This property is a mix of hills and benchland and it produces wonderful wines. On the same property the brothers and sisters of the next older generation make a wonderful Cabernet Sauvignon blend under the Shifflett label. Map E2

Hunnicutt – Calistoga Collectors – Wines: Bordeaux, Burgundy 3524 Silverado Trail North, Saint Helena CA 94574 – www.hunnicuttwines.com – (707) 963–2911 – Hours: 10:00am – 3:30pm Appointment – They are located in a cave north of Saint Helena across from Rombauer. Several other wineries use the same cave complex. Map J

Hyde Estate – Carneros – Wines: Burgundy – 1044 Los Carneros Ave, Napa CA 94558 – www.hydevineyards.com – (707) 265–7626 – Hours: 10:00am – 4:00pm Appointment – Long time Los Carneros grower who finally made their own wines. You can see their building from Carneros Highway. Map C

Inglenook– Formerly Rubicon Estate and before that Niebaum Coppola and before that Inglenook, meaning a safe place – Napa Italian Style with History owned by the Coppolas – Wines: Chardonnay, Cabernet Sauvignon, Merlot, Cabernet Franc, Syrah, Blanc de Blanc, Rosé, Sauvignon Blanc, Pinot Noir, Zinfandel, Rubicon – 1991 St Helena Highway (Highway 29). Rutherford 94573 www.inglenook. com – (707) 968-1161 Hours: 10:00am – 5:00pm Appointment – Tours – This is the premier winery of the family of the movie director Francis Ford Coppola and his wife Eleanor, where they produce their best estate wines. It includes a spacious tasting room, an elegant gift shop and an espresso bar, which is a wonderful place to relax amid a day of tasting with some chocolate or a cigar, which they sell in the cafe. You can sail a boat in the fountain making this among the most family–friendly wineries in Napa. The staff is excellent and the whole feeling is gracious and special. It was the center of the Niebaum Estate that Francis gradually reassembled. 'Rubicon' comes from the story of Julius Caesar returning from Gaul after his victories there. His enemies rigged the laws against him so crossing the Rubicon River into Italy would make him a rebel. Once he crossed, there was no going back. Once Francis made his first wine there was no going back. Map F3

Ink Grade Vineyards – Tasting Pavillion Across from V Sattui – Wines: Sauvignon Blanc, Merlot, Cabernet Sauvignon – 699 St Helena Hwy, St Helena, CA 94574 – www.inkgrade.com – (707) 200-9099 – Hours: 10:00am – 3:30pm Appointment – These grapes were orginally used by Burgess, but the new owner split it off into its own winery label, and transformed a tasting room into a place for an immerive experience. Map F3

Italics Winegrowers – Coombsville Cave – Closed – Map D

J Gregory – City of Napa – Wines: Bordeaux and Burgundy – 1819 El Centro Ave, Napa CA 94558 – www.jgregorywines.com (707) 474–2149 – Hours: 10:00am – 4:00pm Appointment – Tasting room. Map A1

J Moss – Corporate Park – Wines: Bordeaux and Burgundy, General French – 901 Enterprise Way, Suite B, Napa 94558 – www.jmosswines.com – (707) 647–3388 – Appointment. Map A1 Zone 1, Does not appear on map

JaM Cellars - Downtown Napa next to the Andaz Hotel - 1460 1st St, Napa, CA 94559 - jamcellars.com - (707) 265-7577 - JaM is a big brand and a force in the downtown, as owners of two local theaters. They also have a tasting among the vineyards in an old church building on Thompson Road in Los Caneros. Map A2

James Cole Estate Winery – Small Oak Knoll District – Wines: Chardonnay, Malbec, Cabernet Sauvignon – 5014 Silverado Trail Napa CA 94558 – www.jamescolewinery.com - 707) 251–9905 Hours: 10:00am – 5:00pm Appointment – They are located at the intersection of the Silverado Trail and Oak Knoll Road, owned by a local family. The tasting is casual, the staff friendly and knowledgeable, and the wines good. The building and tasting room are elegant and understated. When the Highway 29 wineries are busy, you might find a nicer experience here, away from the crowds. Map E3

Jarvis Vineyards – Remarkable Cave Winery – Wines: Chardonnay, Cabernet Sauvignon and Bordeaux varietals – 2970 Monticello Road Napa CA 94558 – www.jarviswines.com – (800) 255–5280 – Hours: 11am – 4:30 Appointment with tour The winery is inside their beautiful cave and tasting there is a unique experience, as you cross over a stream that runs through the caves so bring a sweater. They have an event space filled with museum quality crystals. On the drive watch for an outcropping that looks like a man smoking a pipe. Map E3

Jericho Canyon - Calistoga - 3322 Old Lawley Toll Rd, Calistoga, CA 94515 - www.jerichocanyonvineyard.com - (707) 942-9665 - This family owned and operated winery is tucked against the eastern palisades off the Silverago Trail just outside downtown Calistoga. They make Cabernet, Sauvignon Blanc and a Rose. A very pretty estate that is tucked away so allow extra time to get there. Map K

Jessup Cellars – Downtown Yountville Tasting Room – Wines: Chardonnay, Rosé, Merlot, Zinfandel, Cabernet Sauvignon, Blends, Petite Syrah, Zinfandel Port – 6740 Washington Street Yountville CA 94599 – www.jessupcellars.com – (707) 944–8523 – Hours: 10:00am – 6:pm – They are popular with small tour companies so their tasting room can get filled up fast, but it is still fun. Some wonderful wines and the space doubles as an art gallery. Map E5

John Anthony Vineyards – Downtown Napa – Wines: Bordeaux and Burgundy – 1440 First Street, Napa CA 94558 – www.johanthonyvineyards.com – (707) 265–7711 – Hours: 10am-8pm. They also offer vineyard tastings in their 'church'. Map A2 Zone 2

Joseph Cellars – Calistoga – Wines: Bordeaux – 4455 St Helena Highway Calistoga CA 94515 – www.josephcellars.com – (707) 942–999 – Hours: 10:00am – 4:30pm Appointment – This is a small winery with their cave behind them on Highway 29 just south of downtown Calistoga. Map K

Joseph Phelps Vineyards – Beautiful Secluded Valley – Wines: Cabernet Sauvignon, Sauvignon Blanc, Syrah, Viognier, Dessert Wine – 200 Taplin Road Saint Helena CA 94574 – www.jpvwines.com – (707) 967–3720 – Hours: Appointment – They are in a gorgeous valley off the Silverado Trail. They offer seminars. They were the first Napa winery to create a Bordeaux–style blend. Navigation Tip: Taplin Road is on the east side of the Silverado Trail north of the intersection with Zinfandel Lane. It is a tight turn and the road is narrow so take your time. Map G3

Judd's Hill Winery – Custom Crush – Wines: Cabernet Sauvignon, Petite Syrah, Chardonnay, Merlot, Zinfandel, Pinot Noir 2332 Silverado Trail Napa CA 94558 – www.juddshill.com - (707) 255–2332 – Hours: 10:00am – 5:00pm Appointment - They pour their own wines, but they are also a custom facility. Unlike many that exist throughout wine country they work with clients as small as one barrel, which is tempting. They are near the corner of the Silverado Trail and Trancas Street. Map E3

Kelham Vineyards and Winery – True Napa – Wines: Cabernet Sauvignon, Sauvignon Blanc, Merlot, Chardonnay, Port - 360 Zinfandel Lane Saint Helena CA 94574 – www.kelhamvineyards.com – (707) 963–2000 – Hours: Appointment – This is a gracious, charming family run winery. They do seated tastings outside on a remarkable patio. They also taste inside where there is a unique art collection centered on wine labels. The tasting is done by the family, including the two winemakers. They are unusual because they allow the wines to age for many years before they release them, to produce the most spectacular results. This is not a tasting you want to rush. In 2021 they introduced an innovative multi-media wine and food pairing that is a remarkable experience people will remember fondly for years. They have beautiful architecture and gardens. Map F3

Kelleher Family Vineyard – At the Brix Restaurant – Wines: Bordeaux and Burgundy – PO Box 111 Oakville, Ca 94562 – www.kelleherwines.com – 866 531–2580 – Hours: Appointment This family owns Yountville's Brix Restaurant, their vineyards are beyond the back patio overlooking the valley floor. They pour at the edge of the vineyards and there is a bonus. You can arrange for your lunch, or a paring to accompany the tasting. Do not worry, the tables have umbrellas to protect you from Napa's abundant sunshine. Map   E2

Kelly Fleming Winery – SOLD Calistoga – Wines: Bordeaux and Burgundy Probably not seeing guests – www.kellyflemingwines.com – (707) 942–6849 – Hours: 10:00 am – 3:00pm Monday–Sold in 2024 – Located down a long county road off the Silverado Trail, this Tuscan style winery is set against a hillside, with a long tunnel bored into the native rock. Kelly Fleming likes having a team of mostly women winemakers and they produce a lovely product. Map K

Keenan Vineyards – Spring Mountain – Cabernet Blends and a variety of other grapes – 3660 Spring Mountain Rd, St Helena, CA 94574 – www.keenanwinery.com – (707) 963-9177 – They are located halfway up Spring Mountain Road, and down a long driveway. The winery was constructed in the 1800's and from the comfortable and tasting room there are vineyards views. The wines are good and the hospitality down to earth and knowledgeable. Family owned and the long-time owner is hands on. Plan extra time for the ride because you don't want to have to rush in the final parts the narrow drive. Map H

Keever Winery – A small Yountville family winery with great views – Wines: Bordeaux and Burgundy Blends – P.O. Bo 2906, Yountville, CA 94559 www.keevervineyards.com – (707) 944–0910 – Hours: 11:00am – 2:30pm Appointment – A lovely hillside winery surrounded by vineyards south of Yountville. They are a small production, high-quality winery run by the family. Map E2

Kenzo Estate – Remarkable Cave Winery – Wines: Bordeaux & Burgundy – 3200 Monticello Road Napa CA 94558 – www.kenzoestate.com – (707) 815-6736 – Hours: Appointment – This is a beautiful estate in the eastern hills of southeast Napa. It was once the Olympic equestrian center before it was bought by Mr. Kenzo, a Japanese Billionaire, so it still has horse trails. It is an elegant winery building and cave complex with solid, well made wines. Map E3

Kenefick Ranch Vineyard & Winery – A small family winery just south of downtown Calistoga at the base of the eastern palisades – Wines: Sauvignon Blanc, Cabernet Franc, Grenache Blanc, Petite Sirah – 2200 Pickett Rd, Calistoga, CA 94515s – www.kenefick-ranch.com – (707) 942-6175 – Hours: Appointment – This is a famiy run business combining the first and second generations. They do interesting varietals. Map K

K Laz Wines – Downtown Yountville Wine Retail Outlet and Tasting lounge – Wines: Bordeaux and Burgundy Blends, General French – 6484 Washington St Suite C, Yountville, CA 94599 –www.klazwinecollection.com – (707) 415–5040 – Hours: 10:00am – 5:00pm. Map E5

Krupp Brothers Estate – two locations: Estate winery & Oxbow tasting room – Wines: Cabernet Sauvignon, Chardonnay- The Estate Address: 1094 Hardman Ave, Napa, CA 94558 – www.kruppbrothers.com – (707) 225–2276 – Hours: Appointment They taste at their lovely Tuscan style estate just north of the city of Napa. Although there are vineyards on the site, many of their best grapes come from the Stagecoach Vineyards high up on Atlas Peak, that the brothers developed in the 1990's. Even though they sold the Stagecoach vineyards to Gallo. Map Downtown A2 Zone 4, in the Oak Knoll E3

Kuleto Estate Family Vineyards – Top of Sage Canyon – Wines: Cabernet Sauvignon, Sangiovese, Syrah, Pinot Noir, Chardonnay – 2470 Sage Canyon Road Saint Helena CA 94574 – www.kuletoestate.com – (707) 963–9750 – Hours: Appointment – It is a long ride out Sage Canyon Road to the gate. The winding driveway up has 12 convex mirrors at the hairpin turns. The location is cool with the vineyards perched on top of the mountains and the buildings are unique, with a great mix of muscularity and grace. Map F5

La Sirena – The Wines of Heidi Peterson Barrett for Collectors Wines: An eclectic collection with a Cabernet at its core – www.lasirenawine.com – (707) 942–1105 Hours: Appointment

Ladera Vineyards – Calistoga – Wines: Bordeaux and Burgundy– 3942 Silverado Trail North Calistoga, CA 94515 (707) 965-2445 www.laderavineyards.com – (707) 968–9900 – Their previous winery was sold to Cade and renamed Vineyard 13. But the label endures, and the wines are being made at the Brasswood custom crush facility, and they do their tastings there. They also do seated tastings at their location on the Silverado Trail just south of Larkmead Road. However, that site requires climbing many steps. Map J

Lail Vineyards – Collectors – Wines: Bordeaux and Burgundy – PO Box 249, Rutherford, CA 94573 – www.lailvineyards.com – (707) 968–9900 – Hours: Appointment. Map I. Not on map

Laird Family Estate – Oak Knoll Copper Pyramid – Wines: Pinot Grigio, Chardonnay, Syrah, Cabernet Sauvignon, Merlot 5055 Solano Ave. Napa CA 94558 – www.lairdfamilyestate.com (707) 257–0360 Hours: 10:00am – 5:00pm Appointment This pyramid building with a surrounding patio sits in Oak Knoll AVA, but the Laird family owns vineyards in various parts of Napa. The highly active winery you see through the window is their custom crush facility that serves numerous other wineries. The Laird family has a long history in Napa. Map E3

Laura Michael Wines – Previously called Zahtila, same owners Wines: Cabernet Sauvignon, Zinfandel, Chardonnay – 2250 Lake County Highway, Calistoga CA 94515 – www.lauramichaelwines.com – (707) 942–9251 – 10:00am – 5:00pm Appointment – This small, charming outisde downtown Calistoga makes nice wines and pours them with that friendly inclusiveness that makes Calistoga shine. The name comes from first names of the two owners. Map K

Larkmead Vineyards – Calistoga Ultra–Premium – Wines: Cabernet Sauvignon, Merlot, Sauvignon Blanc – 1100 Larkmead Lane Calistoga CA 94515 – www.larkmead.com – (707) 942–0167 – Hours: 10:00am – 4:00pm Appointment – This white winery is easy to spot as you travel north on Highway 29 above Saint Helena. They are a quality producer and the family, which has long ties in San Francisco, has owned the vineyards for many years. They do a lovely tasting in their salon with great views of the vineyards. Map J

Leto Cellars – Corporate Park – Wines: Bordeaux, Burgundy 759 Technology Way, Napa CA 94558 – www.letocellars.com – (707) 259–5386 – Hours: Appointment Map A1 Does not appear on maps

Lewis Cellars – Oak Knoll Collectors – Wines: Bordeaux and Burgundy – 4101 Big Ranch Rd, Napa CA 94558 – www.lewiscellars.com – (707) 255–3400 – Hours: Appointment – They recently got hign scores and are priced accordingly, although the tasting is understated. Map E1

Lokoya – Spring Mountain Premium Cabernet Sauvignon – 3787 Spring Mountain Road Saint Helena CA 94574 – www.lokoya.com – (707) 948-1968 – Hours: Appointment – This is an extraordinary building with a story, built many years ago from stone by a hermit winemaker, that is worth the ride by itself. The the Jackson family did a dramatic renovation to reflect the ultra-premium nature of the wines. Map H

Long Meadow Ranch – Tasting Room at the Farmstead Restaurant Wines: Cabernet Sauvignon, Sauvignon Blanc, Sangiovese, Ranch House Red, Olive Oil, Beef Jerky. 738 Main Street St Helena CA 94574 – www.longmeadowranch.com – (707) 963–4555 – Hours: 11:00am–6:00pm The main property is a large-acre hillside farm, ranch and winery, producing not only wine and olive oil, but also produce and meats. Map G5

Louis M. Martini Winery – Great Wines in Central Napa – Wines: Cabernet Sauvignon, Zinfandel, Chardonnay, Merlot, Cabernet Franc, Syrah, Petite Syrah – 254 St Helena Highway South (Highway 29). Saint Helena 94574 (800) 321–9463 - www.louismartini.com – Hours: 10:00am – 6:00pm – Appointment – This winery started just after Prohibition ended, and then in the third generation it was sold to their long time family friends the Gallos who poured big money into this site. They produced a destination winery, with spacious tasting bars, gorgeous reserve room and an expansive tasting garden. The wines have always been good, and they are centrally located. The building includes spaces for large groups. Map G2

Macauley Vineyard – Downtown Saint Helena Tasting Room for Big Oakville Cabernets – Wines: Burgundy, Outliers – 1309 Main Street, Saint Helena 94574 –www.macauleyvineyard.com (707) 963–1863 Hours: Appointment – In the 2nd generation. Map G5

Madonna Estate – Carneros – Wines: Pinot Grigio, Chardonnay, Pinot Noir, Merlot, Dolcetto, Cabernet Sauvignon, Riesling, Gewürztraminer, Muscat Canelli – 5400 Old Sonoma Road Napa CA 94559 www.madonnaestate.com – (707) 255–8864 – Hours: 10:00am – 5:00pm – This is an organic family winery with dry farmed vineyards, which is unusual. They have a picnic area just off the road. They are convenient from San Francisco which makes them a popular tour bus stop. They are 3rd and 4th generation Italian American winemakers, and they make remarkably good wines that are properly priced. If there is no tour bus in their lot they are worth a visit. Map C

Madrigal Family – CLOSED Calistoga – 3718 North Saint Helena Highway, Calistoga CA 94515 – www.madrigalfamilywinery.com – . This long time grower was sold to Hundred Acre Vineyards - Map J

Mahoney Vineyards – Los Carneros – Wines: Chardonnay, Pinot Noir – 1134 Dealy Lane, Napa CA 94558 – www.carneroswinecompany.com – (707) 253–9464 – Hours: Appointment - Map D

Marita's Vineyard – Small Coombsville Collectors – Wines: Bordeaux – PO Box 4164, Napa CA 94558 – www.maritasvineyard.com – (707) 259–5313 – Hours: Appointment – This is a very small producer of excellent wines from the hills of southeastern Napa. The vines are tended by the winemakers and they produce lovely flavors with great depth. Map D

Markham Vineyards – Rock and Roll – Wines: Merlot, Cabernet Sauvignon, Sauvignon Blanc, Chardonnay – 2812 St Helena Highway North (Highway 29) Saint Helena CA 94574 – www.markhamvineyards.com – (707) 963–5292 – Hours: 11:00am – 5:00pm Appointment – This winery is located north of downtown Saint Helena. It is a well–known producer of middle of the road wines. They have a spacious tasting room with an art gallery featuring photography of Rock and Roll icons from the 60's and 70's, a nice gift shop and some good, well–priced wines. Their staff is always pleasant, and the grounds and patio are a pleasant place to hang out. Map J

Maroon Winery – Small Family Coombsville – Wines: Bordeaux, Zinfandel – 3565 Hagen Road Napa, CA 94558 – www.maroonwines.com   (707) 257–3040 – Hours: Appt – The drive at the NV Country Club. Map D

Marston Family – Spring Mountain Collectors – Wines: Bordeaux , Burgundy – Saint Helena CA 94574 – www.marstonfamilyvineyard.com – (707) 963–8490 – Hours: Appt. Map H - Not on map

Martin Estate – Collectors – Wines: Cabernet Sauvignon Blends Post Office Box 390 Rutherford, CA 94573 – www.martinestate.com (707) 967–0400 – The winery is on Conn Creek Road in Rutherford across from Frog's Leap. It sits behind trees in a long stone building that dates to the founding of the Beaulieu Winery in the late 1800's, for which this was originally constructed. But BV outgrew it in a couple of years. It served as a residence until the current owners restored it, built a winery on the ground floor and planted the small area along the side of the Conn Creek with vines. Map F4

Materra / Cunat – Oak Knoll – Wines: Bordeaux and Burgundy – 4326 Big Ranch Road, Napa CA 94558 – www.materrawines.com (707) 224–4900 – Hours: 10:00am – 4:30pm - This sits on the corner of Big Ranch Road and Oak Knoll Cross Road in an area known for being able to grow everything. This is a new winery and part of the facility serves custom clients. The wines are well made. Map E2

Matthiasson Winery – A wide variety of nicely priced wines west of downtown Napa –3175 Dry Creek Rd. Napa, CA 94558 – www.matthiasson.com – (707) 637-4877 – The tastings are often outside in area next to the building. There is nothing fancy about the place, but they make highly respected, solidly good wine from multiple varietals at a reasonable price compared to many in Napa. The staff is casual and knowledgeable and fun to work with. Map B

Maxville Lake – Chiles Valley – Wines: Bordeaux and Petite Syrah – 4105 Chiles Pope Valley Rd, Saint Helena CA 94574 – www.maxvillelakewines.com – (707) 965–9378 – Hours: 10:00am – 4:00 pm Appointment – This is a very modern winery on a thousand acres in this Chiles Valley in the hills of eastern Napa. Vines have been planted there since the early 1970's and the new owner has invested in a new winery and hospitality center that overlooks their lake. They have an excellent wine making team. Map F5

Mayacamas – Ultra Premium Tasted in Downtown Napa or at the Estate – Wines: Bordeaux and Burgundy – Downtown 1256 First Street Napa, CA 94559 – Estate 1155 Lokoya Road, Napa CA 94558 – www.mayacamas.com – (707) 224–4030 – Hours: Downtown 11am-6m (Check Website) – In 2017 their historic winery building in the Mayacamas mountains burned down. They have rebuilt and tasting are possible at the estate, although it is much less convenient than the downtown location. Map A1 Zone, Estate Map B

McKenzie-Mueller Vineyards & Winery – Los Carneros Family – Wines: Pinot Noir, Chardonnay – 2530 Las Amigas Rd, Napa, CA 94559 – www.mckenziemueller.com – (707) 252-0186 Hours: Appointment – These native Napans have been involved in wine making for more than fifty years. They produce 2000 cases yearly of authentic Los Carneros wines. Map C

Melka Estates – Collectors Saint Helena – Wines: Bordeaux and Burgundy, General French – P.O. Box 509 Saint Helena, CA 94574 – www.melkaestates.com – (707) 963–6008 – Hours: Appointment – Philippe Melka is a prominent consulting winemaker and the winery is located at the intersection of the Silverado Trail and Deer Park Rd. Map J

Mending Wall – Wines: Bordeaux and Burgundy Blends, General French – 3730 Silverado Trail N, St Helena, CA 94574 – www.mendingwall.com – (707) 709–4200 – Hours: 10:00am – 3:00pm Appointment – This custom crush facility and tasting room features the wines of the senior wine maker, Thomas Rivers Brown. It is a stylish tasting room with stellar wines. Map J

Merryvale Vineyards – Downtown Winery – Wines: Sauvignon Blanc, Chardonnay, Merlot, Cabernet Sauvignon, Fortified Dessert Wine, Zinfandel, Pinot Noir – 1000 Main Street Saint Helena CA 94574 – www.merryvale.com – (707) 963–7777 – Hours: 10:00am – 6:30pm Appointment – The building was once owned by the Mondavi family during the days of bulk winemaking. It sits beside the railroad tracks, and they would pull tanker cars up to the barrel room and fill them up. Now that grand room, lined with old wooden tanks is used for events, with a banquet table running the length of it. They have a big tasting bar, that is open late compared to their neighbors. The tasting room is adjacent to the winery's tank room and you can see the line of stainless tanks through the doorway. They are on the south edge of downtown Saint Helena and next Pizzeria Tra Vigne and Gott's Roadside. Map G2

Merus Wines – Premium Tucked in the Hills – Wines: Bordeaux and Burgundy – 424 Crystal Springs Road Saint Helena, CA 94574 – www.meruswines.com – (707) 251–5551 – Hours: 10:00am – 4:00pm Monday– Sunday Appointment – Map J

Migration Winery – Los Carneros – Wines: Chardonnay, Pinot Noir 1451 Stanly Lane Napa, CA 94559 – (707) 415-2298 – www.migrationwines.com – Hours: 10:00am – 3:30pm Appointment – This is a larger facility connected with Duckhorn, thus the 'fowl' reference. It is tucked off by itself, although you can see it from Highway 29. It is next door to the site of a new Stanly Ranch hotel. Map C

Miner Family Vineyards – Great Views – Wines: Chardonnay, Viognier, Sauvignon Blanc, Cabernet Sauvignon, Pinot Noir, Merlot, Syrah, Zinfandel, Sangiovese, Rosato. 7850 Silverado Trail Oakville CA 94558 – www.minerwines.com – (707) 944–9500 Hours: 11:00am to 5:00pm – This is a fun winery with an interesting list made from grapes they source both inside and outside Napa. They have great views from the front patio and a friendly staff. You can see the entire winery from the tasting room and they have a cave for events. Map F4

Mi Sueno Winery – Corporate Tasting Room – Wines: Bordeaux and Burgundy – 910 Enterprise Way Suite M Napa, CA 94558 – www.misuenowinery.com – (707) 258–6358 – Appointment

Monticello Cellars – Corely Family in Oak Knoll – Wines: Bordeaux and Burgundy – 4242 Big Ranch Road Napa CA 94558 – www. CorleyFamilyNapaValley.com – (707) 253–2802 – Hours: 10:00am – 4:30pm They are in the southern part of the valley just north of Downtown Napa, in the Oak Knoll district, nearby Materra and Trefethen. They are also the site of a scaled replica of the home of Thomas Jefferson, Monticello, although the bar tastings are done in a facing building, they do a high end tasting in the cellar under the Monticello replica building. They have a nice picnic area so reserve your table. Map E2

Morlet Family Vineyards – Collectors – Wines: Bordeaux and Burgundy – 2825 St Helena Highway, St Helena, CA 94574 – www.morletwines.com – (707) 967–8690 – Hours: Appointment – Owned by a couple. They make remarkable wines in their 1880 stone building just north of Saint Helena. Map J

Mumm Napa – Sparkling Wines and Great Photo Gallery – Wines: Sparkling and Still Wines. 8445 Silverado Trail Rutherford 94573 – www.mummnapa.com – (707) 967–7700 – Hours: 10:00am – 5:00pm Appointment – This fun winery pours interesting sparkling wines inside their tasting room and outside on their expansive patio, with great views and a central location. They have a fantastic photography museum, with rotating exhibits and they offer tours. Even though most of their vineyards are to the south in Los Carneros, the founding winemaker chose this site for its beauty and reminded everyone that he had trucks to move the grapes. Map F4

Napa Cellars – Friendly Winery – Wines: Chardonnay, Sauvignon Blanc, Zinfandel, Cabernet Sauvignon, Merlot, Pinot Noir, Syrah. Picnic tables – 7481 Saint Helena Highway, Hwy 29 Oakville CA 94562 – www.NapaCellars.com – (707) 944–2565 - Hours: 10:00am – 6:00pm –They allow guests to bring their lunch and use their picnic tables. It is in an easy location just north of Yountville and they are open to 6 pm. They enjoy a loyal clientele and that makes the place a lot of fun. Map E1

Neal Family Vineyards – Howell Mountain – Wines: Cabernet Sauvignon, Sauvignon Blanc, Petite Syrah, Zinfandel – 716 Liparita Road Angwin CA 94508 – www.nealvineyards.com – (707) 965–2800 – Hours: 10:00am – 5:00pm Appointment - This is a small production, high quality, BioDynamic, state of the art winery. They are a little bit of a drive up the mountainous winding roads, but if you are an enthusiast then it is worth it. Like many small wineries, they offer a tour. Map I

Neyers Vineyards – Up a Winding Road – Wines: Bordeaux and Burgundy – 2153 Sage Canyon Road, Saint Helena 94574 www.neyersvineyards.com – (707) 963–8840 – Hours: 10:00am – 5:00pm Tuesday–Saturday Appointment – This small family winery is tucked up the narrow canyon that was hit by fires in 2017, but it has recovered well. Map F5

Newton Vineyard – *Note: CLOSED 2025 The 2020 Glass Fire damaged their buildings and gardens on Spring Mt. They moved their winery and tasting room to Calistoga* – They are highly respected winery owned by the same company that owns Domaine Chandon. Wines: Chardonnay, Merlot, Cabernet Sauvignon, Cabernet Franc, Petit Verdot – 1171 Tubbs Ln, Calistoga, CA 94515 – www. newtonvineyard.com – (707) 204-7423 Hours: Appt. Map K1

Nichelini Winery – Chiles Valley – Wines: Sauvignon Blanc, Chardonnay, Zinfandel, Petite Syrah, Cabernet Sauvignon, Primitivo – 2950 Sage Canyon Rd Saint Helena CA 94574 – www.nicheliniwinery.com – (707) 963–0717 – Hours: 10:00am – 5:00pm Appointment – This is one of Napa's oldest family wineries perched on a hillside in the Chiles Valley (rhymes with tiles). It is a twenty–minute ride from the Silverado Trail They make wonderful wine in a great location. When you see where they are and realize that the original settlers did much of this work by hand, it is amazing. There are some interesting stories about how the family handled Prohibition. That area was hit by fires in 2020, but they were well prepared to save their property and escaped without damage. Map F5

Nickel and Nickel – Oakville Charm – Wines: Chardonnay, Cabernet Sauvignon, Merlot, Syrah, Zinfandel – 8164 St Helena Highway (Highway 29) Oakville CA 94558 – www.nickelandnickel.com – (707) 967–9600 – Hours: 10:00am – 3:00pm Appointment   They have beautiful buildings and gardens, and a great tour and sit–down tasting of their single vineyard wines. They are associated with Far Niente. You should do the tour if you can. The winery sits across from the Robert Mondavi Winery and you can spot it from the horses grazing in front. Map F5

Neiman Cellars – Collectors – Napa – www.neimancellars.com (707) 322–7478 – Hours: Appointment – info@neimancellars.com – 600 cases of wine made by Drew Neiman. Does not appear on map

Oakville Ranch – The Hills of Eastern Oakville – 7781 Silverado Trail, Napa, CA 94558 – www.oakvilleranch.com – (707) 944-9665 – Even though the address is on Silverado Trail, that is just where the private road begins that leads up the eastern slopes of the Vaca Mountains where several estates make their home. This beautiful, expansive, organic, solar powered, 370-acre property, a thousand feet above the valley floor, is a marvel of nature with great views.

Amazingly they are not 'over the top' expensive and the visit includes an ATV tour of the property so wear practical shoes. Make your appointment in advance and allow yourself extra travel time. Mapa F5

Oakville Market – **The 1881 Napa Tasting Room** – This is next to the Market and owned by the same people – Wines: A variety of Napa's most famous wines avaiable by the taste or glass – 7856 St Helena Highway, Oakville – www.1881napa.com – (707) 944–8802 – Hours: Open to the public 7am - 6pm. Map F3

O'Brien Family Vineyard – South of Yountville – Wines: Chardonnay, Merlot, Bordeaux Blend called Seduction – 1200 Orchard Ave. Napa CA 94558 – www.obrienfamilyvineyard.com (707) 252–8463 – Hours: 10am – 5pm Tuesday–Sunday Appointment – This is a family winery on a pretty property convenient to downtown Napa. They do a good tour, romantic and personal and a wine tasting sitting in signt of the vineyards. The winery equipment is right next to the tasting room. The wines are quite special, as are the people who make it. Their vineyards are Biodynamic/Organic. Map E2

Odette Estate – Pretty Winery in Stags Leap – Wines: Bordeaux and Burgundy – They are connected to Plumpjack and Cade. 5998 Silverado Trail Napa CA 94558 – www.OdetteEstate.com – (707) 224–7533 – Hours: 10:30 – 4:00pm – This was the former Steltzner property which was bought by the Plumpjack group. It was transformed into a very socially appealing space, elegant, spacious, with indoor and outdoor tastings, while looking out over the vineyards. Map E3

Olivia Brion Winery – Wines: Burgundy and Rose – www.oliviabrion.com – (707) 287–2870 – Hours: Appointment – A very small winery project with an interesting story. Does not appear on maps

One Hope Winery – Rutherford Winemaking as Philantropy – Wines: A variety of still & sparkling – www.onehopewine.com – 8305 St Helena Hwy, Napa, CA 94558 – Half their profits go to good causes but tastings are very limited. Map F3

Opus One Winery – An International Standard – Wines: Two Bordeaux style Blends – 7900 St Helena Highway (Highway 29). Oakville 94562   www.OpusOneWinery.com – (707) 944–9442 Hours: 10:00am – 4:00pm Appointment – Tour – Opus One is found on wine lists around the world and sure to impress any client that you are entertaining. This extraordinary building looks like an Incan temple, a white exterior submerged into green lawns surrounded by vines which are grown in the European method. The shape actually mimics a wine glass. It was started in the 1970's by the Baron von Rothschild and Robert Mondavi to combine European technology and California grapes. They produce one red wine made from the five Bordeaux varietals. Schedule tours well in advance. Map F3

Orin Swift Cellars –Elegant Downtown Tasting Room Saint Helena – Wines: Cabernet, Syrah. 1321 Main Street St Helena (Highway 29) CA 94574 www.orinswift.com – (707) 976–9179. Map G5

O'Shaughnessy Estate Winery – Howell Mountain – Wines: Cabernet Sauvignon, Merlot. 1150 Friesen Dr Angwin CA 94508 www.oshaughnessywinery.com – (707) 965–2898 – Hours: Appointment – This is a beautiful, isolated winery started in 2000 with a unique curved cave. If you are an enthusiast, it is worth the drive. They email directions through the a maze of small roads. Map I

Otra Vez Winery – Wines: Cabernet Sauvignon – 2280 Greenwood Ave, Calistoga CA 94515 – www.otravezwinery.com – (707) 942–4310 Hours: Appointment – This is a project by Vincent Arroyo, whose originally winery you pass on the way here. Very small production and high quality. Map K

Outpost Wines – Howell Mountain – Wines: Zinfandel, Grenache, Petite Syrah, Cabernet Sauvignon. 2075 Summit Lake Dr. Angwin CA 94508 – www.outpostwines.com – (707) 965–1718 Hours: Appointment – On the top of Howell Mountain looking across at Spring Mountain. While they produce some wonderful wines, they are known just as much as a crush facility for some of Napa's hot labels. It is quite a ride to the top, but the views and the wines are great. Get them to send you directions. Map I

Ovid – Collectors – Wines: Bordeaux Style – 255 Long Ranch Road, Saint Helena CA 94574 – www.ovidnapavalley.com – (707) 963–3850 – Hours: Appointment – This ultra-premium winery overlooks the Napa Valley. They are on the eastern ridge of the valley so allow extra time to get there up the narrow, winding road. Map F5

Palladian Estate Winery – Saint Helena – 690 Meadowood Lane St. Helena, CA 94574 – www.palladianwine.com – (707) 963–7106 – Hours: 10:00am – 4:30pm Monday – Friday Appointment – This is a rustic winery just outside Saint Helena next to the Meadowood Resort that makes good wines and pours them outside. G3

Palmaz Vineyards – Big Coombsville Caves – Wines: Cabernet Sauvignon Blends, Riesling, Chardonnay, Muscat Cannelli - 4029 Hagen Road Napa CA 94559 – www.palmazvineyards.com – (707) 226-5587 – This five story cave winery is east of downtown in an area with numerous cave wineries. The tasting area sits high on the hillside. Allow two hours for the tour and tasting. Map D

Paoletti Vineyards – Italian Style – Wines: Bordeaux and Super Tuscan blends, Nero d' Avola (Sicilian varietal similar to a new world Shiraz), Rose of Sangiovese – 4501 Silverado Trail Calistoga CA 94515 – www.paolettivineyards.com/ – (707) 942–0689 - Hours:

10:00am–5:00pm Appointment – This is an Italian–style building with with marble sculptures in their cave. The property sits at a curve on the Silverado Trail. They do a casual tasting for a group. They lean towards Italian varietals. Map J

Paradigm Winery – Premium Oakville – Wines: Merlot, Cabernet Sauvignon, Zinfandel, Cabernet Franc – 683 Dwyer Road Oakville CA 94562 – www.paradigmwinery.com – (707) 944–1683 – Hours: Appointment – A respected winery a short ride off Hwy 29. The sign at the beginning of Dwyer Road says, "No Wineries this Road" but it is past their turn so do not believe everything you read! Map F3

Paraduxx – Pair of Ducks – Wines: Bordeaux Blends, Cabernet/Zinfandel, Rhone twist blend. 7257 Silverado Trail Yountville CA 94558 www.paraduxx.com – (707) 945–0890 – Hours: 11:00am–4:00pm by Appointment – This winery sits by itself just off the Silverado Trail north of the intersection with Yountville Cross Road. The name means 'a Pair of Ducks' because it was started by the Duckhorn family to feature their Cabernet/Zinfandel blend. They do a sit–down tasting with a food pairing with indoor and mostly outdoor seating. Map E3

Parallel Winery – Wines: Cabernet Sauvignon – 3125 Saint Helena Highway North (Highway 29) Saint Helena, CA 94574 – www.parallelwines.com – (707) 363–8600 – Hours: 10:00am – 6:00pm Appointment – Not open to public – Taste at the Vintner's Collective or at Brasswood Cellars. Map A2 Zone 2

Patland Estate Vineyards – Caves at Soda Canyon - Wines: Bordeaux and Burgundy – www.patlandvineyards.com – 888 539–4717 Hours: Appointment. Map E3

Peju Province Winery – A Rutherford Jewel – Wines: Sauvignon Blanc, Chardonnay, French Colombard, Syrah, Merlot, Cabernet Franc, Zinfandel, Cabernet Sauvignon, Blends – 8466 St Helena Highway (Highway 29) Rutherford CA 94558 – www.peju.com – (707) 963–3600 – Hours: 10:00am – 6:00pm – The grounds are sprinkled with sculptures and beautiful plantings. The building and rooms are elegant, and the gift shop is unique. The wines are well made and often sourced from Pope Valley. Our suggestion is to visit here early in the day because late in the day they tend to get slammed. Map F3

Pestoni Family – Previously Called Rutherford Grove – Wines: Cabernet Sauvignon, Merlot, Sauvignon Blanc, Petite Syrah, Sangiovese – 1673 Saint Helena Highway Saint Helena CA 94574 – www.pestonifamily.com – (707) 963–0544 – Hours: 10:00am to 4:30pm Appointment – This family first arrived in Napa in the late 1800's. Their most popular wine is their Sauvignon Blanc. The winery is surrounded by their vineyards. Map F3

Piña Cellars – Hillside Winery – Wines: Cabernet Sauvignon, 5 Cabernets from 5 vineyards – 8060 Silverado Trail Rutherford CA 94573 – www.pinacellars.com – (707) 738–932 – Hours: 10:00am – 4:30pm This is a small winery with good wines. The family runs a long–time vineyard management company so they grow good grapes, some of which are on the hillsides just above the small winery. The tasting room is also the barrel room. This is a fun experience and the staff is knowledgeable and often involved in the winemaking process. Map F4

Phifer Pavitt – Collectors – Wines: Bordeaux – 4660 Silverado Trail Calistoga California 94515 –www.phiferpavittwine.com – (707) 942–4787 – A small family winery you can see from the road, Hours: Appointment. Map K

Pine Ridge Vineyards – Stags Leap District – Wines: Chenin Blanc/ Viognier Blend, Rosé, Merlot, Cabernet Franc, Malbec, Cabernet Sauvignon – 5901 Silverado Trail Napa CA 94558 – www.pineridgevineyards.com – (800) 575–9777 – Hours: 10:30am –4:30pm – This winery sits in its own pretty canyon convenient to many other good wineries. The grounds are lovely, although the best sections are reserved for the wine club members. The tasting room is spacious and connected to the barrel cave, which can be seen through the glass doors. Map E3

Plumpjack Winery – Small Winery Big Wines – Wines: Cabernet Sauvignon, Merlot, Chardonnay, Syrah. – 620 Oakville Cross Road Oakville 94558 – www.plumpjack.com – (707) 945–1220 – Hours: 10:00am – 4:00pm Appointment – This is just off Oakville Cross Road, by Silver Oak, B Cellars and Groth. Their sign is at the bottom of the hill. The narrow driveway goes through the vines to this small tasting room. The winery equipment is across the courtyard from the tasting room, so during the crush in late August through November there is a lot to see. The winery's name and emblematic signs have an old English theme related to Shakespeare and Queen Elizabeth. Map F4

Pope Valley Winery – A Long Ride – Wines: Chenin Blanc, Sangiovese, Sangiovese Rosé, Zinfandel, Merlot, Cabernet Sauvignon, Zinfandel Port – 6613 Pope Valley Road CA 94567 – www.popevalleywinery.com (707) 965–1246 – Hours: 11:00am – 5:00pm Thursday – Appointment – This is a small winery 30 minutes over the mountains from the valley floor in the Pope Valley. Many Napa wineries source grapes from this area. This winery dates from 1897. One warning: It gets hot in Pope Valley so save for a cooler day. Map F5

Porter Family Vineyards – East Napa Caves – Wines: Bordeaux and Burgundy, Syrah – 1189 Green Valley Road Napa, CA 94558 – www. porterfamilyvineyards.com – (707) 265–7980 – Hours: Appointment A beautiful winery in the eastern hills that does tastings in their cave which is underneath their vines. Map D

Prager Winery and Port Works – Fun and Cozy – Wines: Late Harvest Riesling, Petit Syrah, Port – 1281 Lewelling Lane Saint Helena CA 94574 – www.pragerport.com – (707) 963–7678 – Hours: Monday–Saturday 10:30–4:30 Appointment – A cozy, eccentric tasting room run by a family with a loyal customer base. Tasting there is like enjoying a favorite port in your uncle's den papered with money. They are behind a large house out of sight of the road. Look for the sign by the driveway. Map G2

Pride Mountain Vineyards – Stunning Views – Wines: Merlot, Cabernet Sauvignon, Cabernet Franc, Viognier, Chardonnay – 4026 Spring Mountain Road Saint Helena CA 94574 – www.pridewines.com – (707) 963–4949 – Hours: Appointment – This beautiful winery sits on the top of Spring Mountain. The Napa Sonoma County line runs through their caves which you tour. They have a great picnic area available to customers. Allow 25 minutes for the steep, winding drive from downtown St Helena. The buildings and caves are neat, and they sell 'I survived my drive to Pride Mountain Tee shirts. Map H

Prime Cellars – Coombsville Winery with Tasting Room in Downtown Napa – Wines: Bordeaux and Burgundy – 974 Franklin Street, Napa CA 94558 – www.primenapa.com – (707) 258–9773 – Hours: 12:00pm – 6:00pm. MapMap E3 Does not appear on map

Prime Solum Winery – Tasting Room – 1021 Atlas Peak Road, Napa – www.primesolum.com – (707) 226–8569 – Hours: 11:00am – 5:00pm – closed Tuesday and Wednesday. Map E3 - Not on map

The Prisoner – Former location of Franciscan – Wines: Bordeaux and Burgundy – www.theprisonerwinecompany.com – 1178 Galleron Rd, St Helena, Ca 94574 – Hours: 10:30am – 4:00pm Appointment – A black, steam punk gulag looking experience, complete with chains, manacles and wine. It can handle large groups in its many different rooms, including its expansive outdoor patio. Map F2

Progeny Winery – Mount Veeder Collectors, Views and Pairings – Wines: Bordeaux and Burgundy – 1032 Mt Veeder Rd, Napa CA 94558 www.progenywinery.com – (707) 252–9466 Hours: 9:00am – 5:00pm Appointment. Map B

Promontory Winery – Ultra–Premium with Great Views – Wines: Big Cab Blends – 1601 Oakville Grade, Oakville CA 94547 www.promontory.wine (707) 944–0125 – Hours: 9:00am to 5:00pm Appointment – concierge@promontory.wine – This is part of the Harlan Group. The tasting is expensive, but the wines, location and the experience are exceptional. Map F3

Quintessa – The Curving Wall – Wines: Bordeaux Blends – 1601 Silverado Trail Rutherford CA 94573 – www.quintessa.com – (707) 967–1601 – Hours: Appointment – This high–end winery focuses on one Bordeaux–style blend that they offer with a food pairing. The tasting/tour is wonderful, and the facility is beautiful. They are easy to spot of the Silverado Trail due to their remarkable building, built in a curve. The caves go directly into the hillside behind the building and the tasting room sits on top like a hat. They have a great staff and they are surrounded by their Biodynamic vineyards. Map F4

Quixote Winery – Most Unique Buildings – Wines: Cabernet Sauvignon, Grenache and Mourvèdre, Petite Syrah – 6126 Silverado Trail Napa CA 94558 – www.quixotewinery.com – (707) 944–2659 – Hours: Appointment – One of Napa's most unique winery buildings. They do a seated tasting that takes 1 to 2 hours for the tour and tasting. Many people come here just to see the building, which was the last project of an Austrian architect with a devoted following. The tile work is remarkable! Map E3

Rarecat Wines – Collectors – They are one of the wineries at Mia Carta in downtown Napa – Wines: Burgundy, General French, Outliers – www.rarecatwines.com – (707) 968–5031. Map A2 Zone 1

Raymond Vineyard – Zinfandel Lane – Wines: Cabernet Sauvignon, Merlot, Chardonnay, Sauvignon Blanc, Petite Syrah, Rosé, Meritage – 849 Zinfandel Lane Saint Helena CA 94574 - ww.raymondvineyards.com – (707) 963–3141 – Hours: 10:00am – 4:00pm – This is owned by Jean Charles Boisset of Burgundy and Napa and he has transformed it into a show piece with diverse educational opportunities and delightful experiences, including the valley's best educational Biodynamic gardens, that is home to goats and chickens. The winery is always changing as the owner invents new experiences and spaces for the visitors to enjoy. The Raymond family was part of the Beringer family, that established this winery after Beringer was sold. Boisset owns Buena Vista and DeLoach in Sonoma. Map F3

Razi Winery – Southern Silverado Trail – Wines: Bordeaux & Burgundy – 3106 Silverado Trail Napa CA 94558 – www.raziwinery.com – (707) 224–4299 – Hours: Monday–Saturday Appointment – A small winery with a yellow sign. Map E3

RD Winery – Asian Style Tasting Room – Wines: A Wide, Eclectic Variety – 3 Executive Way, Napa CA 94558 – www.rdwineryus.com – (707) 259-9446 – Hours: Monday–Saturday by Appointment – This was Napa's first Vietnamese owned winery. Originally the wines were made for export to Vietnam. They produce a variety that are sold through the beautifully designed tasting room or limited distribution. The winery facility was originally owned by a Japanese sake producer and it is large enough that it produces both their own wines while providing services for custom crush clients. They are located south of downtown Napa at a busy commercial intersection near the Napa airport. The site is part of a corporate park filled mostly with companies serving the wine industry. One of the coolest aspects of RD is the variety of wines that they make. Map A1

Realm Cellars – Stags Leap Collectors – Wines: Blends – 5795 Silverado Trail, Napa CA 94558 – www.realmcellars.com – (707) 224–1910 Hours: Appointment – For the serious collector. This was the location of the Hartwell Winery until they sold the site to their winemaker. Map E3

Regusci Winery – Stags Leap District – Wines: Cabernet Sauvignon, Merlot, Zinfandel, and Chardonnay. 5584 Silverado Trail Napa CA 94558 – www.regusciwinery.com – (707) 254–0403 – Hours: 10:00am – 5:00pm – Their stone barrel barn is the oldest winery building in the Stags Leap District. This is a working farm, because the Regusci family manages vineyards for numerous wineries. But they also make their own wine, that comes from the vineyards closest to the barn and tasting room. They have a good staff and a beautiful property. If you want to get the feeling of authentic Napa this is the place to come. They also make olive oil. Map E3

Reid Family Vineyards – Wines: Bordeaux and Burgundy
1020 Borrette Lane, Napa CA 94558 – www.reidfamilyvineyards.com – (707) 252–3195 – Hours: 10:00am – 4:00pm Appointment – reidfamily@reidfamilyvineyards.com – Sitting at the foot of Mt. Veeder, the estate was homesteaded in 1880 as a prune ranch and the original barn, where the tasting happens, remains. The Reids started in 1992, hand-crafting the wines using traditional barrel–to–barrel racking techniques without filtration or fining. They use French and American oak barrels and produce about 1000 cases of each year. Map B

Relic Wine Cellars – Soda Canyon – Cabernet Sauvignon, Merlot, Syrah, Carignane – 2400 Soda Canyon Rd, Napa, CA 94558 – www.relicwines.com – (707) 967-9380 – They are located halfway up this narrow canyon that was devastated in the 2017 fire. Fortunately for the winemaker husband and wife team that own and operate it, the fires bypassed their site. Their winery is outside on a concrete pad two thirds of the way up the ridge, and the wine barrels are in the small cave. The view from the pad where tastings are often conducted are wonderful, as are the wines. Very much worth the ride. They are small so make your appointment well in advance. The grapes come from various vineyards. Map E1

Restoration Hardware – Also known as Ma(i)sonry – Collective Tasting Room and Design Center Downtown Yountville – 6711 Washington Street Yountville CA 94599 – www.maisonry.com – (707) 944–0889 – Hours: 10:00am–7:00pm – This is a combo of a tasting room for small production, high end wineries, a design center and restaurant. The seated tastings are by appointment, although if it is slow consider dropping by and asking for an instant appointment. The tasting is also a chance to see the furniture and design environment. Map E5

Revana Family Vineyard – Ultra Premium by Appointment – Wines: Cabernet Sauvignon, Merlot – 2930 St Helena Highway (Highway 29). North Saint Helena CA 94574 – www.revanawine.com – (707) 967–8814 – Hours: 10:00am – 4:00pm Appointment – This small winery is just off the road above Saint Helena. Map J

Reverie II Winery – Wines: Roussanne, Marsanne, Barbera, Tempranillo, Mountain Cuvee, Cabernet Franc, Cabernet Sauvignon – 264 N Fork Crystal Springs Rd, Deer Park, CA 94576 – www.reveriewine2.com – A charming, small family winery tucked in the hills and assciated with Aonair. Map J

Reynolds Family Winery – Southern Silverado – Wines: Cabernet Sauvignon, Pinot Noir, Chardonna – 3266 Silverado Trail Napa CA 94558 – www.reynoldsfamilywinery.com – (707) 258–2558 – Hours: 10:30am – 4:30pm Appointment – It is a little surprising to find a winery that is this comfortable and relaxed, where the wines are so good, and convenient from downtown Napa. It is a nice combination, right off the Silverado Trail. They have a great side patio overlooking the pond. Their signature wine is called Persistences. Map E3

Rivers Marie Winery – Downtown Calistoga Winery – Wines: Cabernet Sauvignon, Pinot Noir, Chardonnay – 900 Foothill Blvd, Calistoga, CA 94515 – www.www.riversmarie.com – (707) 341-3127 – Hours: Appointment – It is the creation of Thomas Rivers Brown, a wine consultant, and his wife Genevieve Marie Welsh on the site of Marie's original family home. Map F4

Robert Biale Vineyards – Oak Knoll Zinfandels – Wines: Plus Petite Syrah, Barbera, and Sangiovese – 4038 Big Ranch Road Napa CA 94558 – www.robertbialevineyards.com – (707) 257–7555 – Hours: 10:00am – 5:00pm Appointment – This is another of those great Napa families that have growing good grapes for years. They make wonderful Zinfandels, and they offer them with that wonderful, relaxed Napa hospitality. The tasting room is small so most tastings take place outside on the comfortable patio. Map E2

Robert Foley Vineyards – Howell Mountain – Wines: Cabernet Sauvignon, Merlot, Syrah, Chardonnay – 1300 Summit Lake Dr, Angwin, CA 94508 – www.robertfoleyvineyards.com/ – (707) 965-2669 – Hours: They taste by appointment on Thursday, Friday & Saturday at 10:30am – 4:00pm Appointment. Map I

Robert Keenan Winery – Spring Mountain – Wines: Cabernet Sauvignon, Merlot, Zinfandel, Syrah, Chardonnay – 3660 Spring Mountain Road Saint Helena CA 94574 – www.keenanwinery.com – (707) 963–9177 – Hours: 11:00am – 4:00pm Appointment – This winery is about half the way up Spring Mountain. The drive narrow but pretty. The site had a winery on it before Prohibition and the owners did a beautiful job of restoring the building and providing vineyard views. Map H

Robert Mondavi Winery – Note: In 2023 they began a major renovations. They are expected to reopen in 2025. In the interim they opened a hospitality center in downtown Napa called the Tower and Arch at the corner of Soscal St. and Third Street alongside the Napa River, at 930 3rd St, Napa, CA 94559 (888) 766-6328 ext. 2. The only problem is lack of parking, but it is a short walk across the bridge from Main Street. Here is the Oakville Info: A Gracious Estate – Wines: Fumé Blanc, Chardonnay, Pinot Noir, Merlot, Cabernet Sauvignon, Moscato d'Oro, Dry Rosé – 7801 St Helena Highway (Highway 29) – Oakville 94558 – www.robertmondaviwinery.com – (707) 968–2001 – Hours: 10:00am – 5:00pm – Robert Mondavi was Napa's patron saint of marketing, a brilliant personality who was a tremendous influence the area's development. This big, California Mission style winery is almost a pilgrimage for many. It includes some of Napa's best vineyards, midway up the valley with the mountains towering above them. The winery features sculptures, gardens, a gift shop, tours, and both a basic tasting room and the reserve To Kalon room, which is Greek for most beautiful or most high. That is where the big Cabernet Sauvignon wines are poured. These are available both in flights and individually. The winery is said to be on the less desirable western side of Highway 29, the thinking being that it was easier to catch inbound visitors on the eastern side of the road, but clearly, Robert Mondavi overcame this perceived disadvantage. Today the winery is managed by Constellation Brands. Map F3

Robert Sinskey Vineyards – Closed at this location. 6320 Silverado Trail Napa CA 94558 www.robertsinskey.com. Map E3

Robinson Family Vineyards – Stags Leap District – Wines: Cabernet Sauvignon, Merlot – 5880 Silverado Trail Napa CA 94558 – www.robinsonfamilyvineyards.com – (707) 944–8004 - Hours: Appointment – This is a small, family winery down a country road with few signs. They host a limited number of guests. Map E3

Rocca Family Vineyards – South Napa Tasting Room – Coombsville Wines: Bordeaux and Burgundy – 129 Devlin Road, Napa CA 94558 – www.roccawines.com – (707) 257–8467 – Hours: 10:00am – 4:30pm Monday–Saturday Appointment – Their hospitality center is a restored house built in the 1800's down the road from the Napa Airport. So, for those coming to Napa from San Francisco they are very convenient. The wines are from vineyards in Yountville and Coombsville. Map A1

Rombauer Vineyards – Hill Top Perch – Wines: Cabernet Sauvignon, Merlot, Chardonnay, Zinfandel, Port – 3522 Silverado Trail North Saint Helena CA 94574 – www.rombauervineyards.com (707) 963–5170 – Hours: 10:00am – 5:00pm Appointment – Their winery is perched on a hill, on top of a mile of narrow caves. Rombauer is a longtime favorite Chardonnay in restaurants. The family developed the winery while the father was an airline pilot and the mother managed another winery. They are part of the family connected to the book 'The Joy of Cooking'. At the Culinary Institute of America, a few minutes away, they display the many editions from the first, small and simple book. Map J

Round Pond Estate – Rutherford Dust and Olives – Wines: Cabernet Sauvignon, Nebbiolo and then some – 875 Rutherford Road Rutherford CA 94573 – www.roundpond.com – (707) 302–2575 – Hours: 11:00am – 4:00pm Appointment – This family owns hundreds of acres of vines in Rutherford, although most of the grapes are sold to other wineries. They also grow olives and their well–known press is across the way where they do olive tastings. The spectacular winery is at the end of a long palm tree lined drive was created for the small percentage of grapes that they hold onto for their own wines. The tasting room is beautiful with wonderful views of the valley. They also have a commercial kitchen and a tasting bar. Map G3

Rudd – Ultra-Premium and Beautiful – Wines: Cabernet Sauvignon, Chardonnay, Sauvignon Blanc, Blends – 500 Oakville Cross Road Oakville CA 94562 – www.ruddwines.com – (707) 944–8577 Extension 1 – Hours: Tuesday–Saturday Appointment – This is a winery for the collector. The tasting is expensive and so are the wines, but for the serious enthusiast it is a great experience. The gardens are lovely, and the winery is state of the art, even though the tasting is normally limited to the main building, there are extensive caves. Map F4

Rustridge Winery – Chiles Valley – Wines: Bordeaux and Burgundy – 2910 Lower Chiles Valley Road, Saint Helena CA 94574 www.rustridge. com – (707) 965–9353 – Hours: 10:00am – 4:00pm – It is a 25–minute ride from the valley floor to this far end of Chiles Valley (rhymes with miles). Back in the 1950's this was a horse ranch and now the main business is the winery. This area was hit by the Glass Fires in 2020 so check their website for updates and availability. Map F5

Rutherford Hill Winery – Great Views and Tour – Wines: Zinfandel Port, Merlot, Cabernet Sauvignon, Cabernet Franc, Sangiovese, Blends, Petite Verdot, Chardonnay, Syrah, Malbec, Sauvignon Blanc – 200 Rutherford Hill Road Rutherford CA 94558 – www.rutherfordhill.com – (707) 963–1871 – Hours: 10:00am – 5:00pm – They are on a hillside overlooking the valley with great views. They do an excellent tour and the wines are widely distributed. They have picnic tables under hundred–year–old olive trees with views of the valley available for a for a small fee. They also do some tastings there. They have nice indoor and outdoor tasting areas. Check their website for the tour schedule and then make an appointment. They are a popular winery for large corporate groups thanks to their expansive property and large caves. Map G3

Rutherford Ranch – Tucked Away – Wines: Cabernet Sauvignon, Chardonnay, Merlot, Sauvignon Blanc, Zinfandel, White Zinfandel,

Port, Moscato – 1680 Silverado Trail Saint Helena CA 94574 – www.rutherfordranch.com – (707) 967–5120 – Hours: 10:00am – 4:30pm There are two wineries that start with 'Rutherford'. Even though it sits opposite the Conn Creek Winery, it cannot be seen from the Silverado Trail. The tasting room is bright and open. On the hills above is the hotel Auberge du Soleil and above that is the Rutherford Hill Winery. Map G3

Ru Vango– Los Carneros – 1285 Dealy Lane Napa CA 94559 – www.ruvango.com – (707) 253–1615 – Hours: 11:00am – 5:00pm By Appointment – This modern design is fit into a traditional building near Artesa. Their patio looks out at the vineyards and hills. Map C

Saddleback Cellars – Rustic in Oakville – Wines: Pinot Blanc, Pinot Grigio, Chardonnay, Viognier, Merlot, Old Vine Zinfandel, Cabernet Sauvignon – 7802 Money Road Oakville CA 94562 – www.saddlebackcellars.com – (707) 944–1305 – Hours: 10:00am – 4:00pm Appointment – Owned by Nils Venge, a respected consulting winemaker. A small winery on Money Road which is across from the entrance to Silver Oak Winery. Tastings are done outside on picnic tables next to the vines. It is surprising to find such a relaxed, natural winery tucked among all the heavy hitters of Oakville. Map F3

Saintsbury Vineyard – Carneros – Wines: Pinot Noir, Syrah, Chardonnay – 1500 Los Carneros Ave. Napa – www.saintsbury.com – (707) 252–0592 – Hours: Appointment – This long time partnership is widely respected for their Pinot Noir. It is a short distance off Carneros Highway, although not clearly marked so use the street signs and mailbox numbers. They taste at garden tables next to the winery and vineyards. In cold weather they move inside the winery. Map C

Salvestrin Vineyard and Winery – Saint Helena – Wines: Cabernet Sauvignon, Sangiovese, Retaggio (Red Blend), Sauvignon Blanc, Petite Syrah – 397 Main Street Saint Helena CA 94574 – www.salvestrinwinery.com – (707) 963–5105 –
Hours: Appointment – This small family winery is just south of downtown Saint Helena. The tastings are private with nice views of the vineyards. They have been farming Napa since 1932 and released their first vintage in 1994. The wines are good, BioDynamic, and the experience is enjoyable. Map G5

Schramsberg Vineyards – Classic Sparkling Wine Cave Tour Wines: Sparkling Wines and Cabernet Sauvignon – 1400 Schramsberg Road Calistoga CA 94515 – www.schramsberg.com – (707) 942–4558 – Hours: 10:00am–4:00pm Appointment – This is an historic cave winery at the top of a long, winding road. Allow extra travel time and arrive early. The tasting includes the tour and they are set at specific times, so you do not want to be late. The Davies family restored the winery, producing world class sparkling wines in the process. Map J

Schweiger Vineyards – Top of Spring Mountain – Wines: Sauvignon Blanc, Chardonnay, Merlot, Cabernet Sauvignon, Petite Syrah, Port – 4015 Spring Mountain Road Saint Helena CA 94574 – www.schweigervineyards.com – (707) 963–4882 – Hours: 11am – 4:00pm Appointment – This family–run winery is in a beautiful location at the top of Spring Mountain. They have great views and the tasting room sits on rise with great views of the vineyards and the valley beyond. The father grows the grapes, the son makes them into wine, and the daughter runs the tasting room. How cool is that? Map H

Screaming Eagle – Eastern Oakville Cabernet Based Trophy Wine – www.screamingeagle.com – They don't need to be in the directory, but people ask where they are located so...! Map F4

Seavey Vineyard – Conn Valley – Wines: Cabernet Sauvignon, Merlot – 1310 Conn Valley Road Saint Helena 94574 – www.seaveyvineyard.com – (707) 963–8339 – Hours: 10:00am – 4:00pm Appointment – It is a fifteen-minute drive out Conn Valley to the winery. The stone dairy barn that now serves as the winery was built in 1881. The hills are planted with grapes, a beautiful place and a nice tasting. Map I

Sinegal Estate Winery – A newer winery with stylish tasting room on an old property with their own vines – Wines: Cabernet Sauvignon, Sauv Blanc, Chardonnay, Pinot Noir, Rose of Grenache – 2125 Inglewood Ave, St Helena, CA 94574 – www.sinegalestate.com – (707) 244-1187 – Hours: 10:30 – 4:30 pm Appointment – This is a very nice experience in a group tasting area, often outside, so it is beautiful and social with good wines. Map G2

Sequoia Grove Winery – Relaxed and Friendly – Wines: Cabernet Sauvignon, Chardonnay, Syrah – 8338 St Helena Highway (Highway 29). South Rutherford CA 94558 – www.sequoiagrove.com – (707) 944–2945 – Hours: 10:30 – 5:00pm Appointment – They are next to some of the area's most famous wineries and they can hold their own for quality. A charming, relaxed tasting room and a friendly staff. Look for the Sequoia trees next to the building as your landmark. Map F3

Seven Apart – Southern Silverado Trail – 4057 Silverado Trail, Napa, CA 94558 – www.sevenapart.com – (707) 287-1347 Appointment – The wine maker is Andy Erickson, a highly respected and long time member of the wine making community. They are focused on Cabernet. It is new in 2021 and is geared to collectors. However, it is very conveniently located near to the Soda Canyon store. Map E3

Shafer Vineyards – Ultra Premium Stags Leap District Producer – Wines: Chardonnay, Cabernet, Blends – 6154 Silverado Trail Napa CA 94558 – www.shafervineyards.com – (707) 944–2877 – Hours: Tastings at 10am and 2pm Monday–Friday Appointment – Their Hillside Select is a world famous wine that comes from the beautiful canyon that you drive through on the way to the winery. As you drive north on Silverado

Trail there is no sign, just a number. They have a lovely hospitality center perched on a rise that is spacious and light filled. They are one of Napa's great ultra–premium producers that recently changed hands. They have limited seats so plan well in advance. Map E3

Shadybrook Winery – Coombsville with Horses – Wines: Bordeaux and Burgundy – 100 Rapp Lane, Napa CA 94558 – www.shadybrookestate.com – (707) 254–9463 – Hours: 9:00am – 4:00pm Appointment – Charcuterie – In 2020 this was voted the best tasting room by the locals, with its spacious, comfortable patio and big pours. It is part of a property with commercial stables and trail rides through the vineyards. Map D

Sherwin Family Vineyards – Spring Mountain – Wines: Cabernet Sauvignon, Blends – 4060 Spring Mountain Road Saint Helena CA 94574 www.sherwinfamilyvineyards.com – (707) 963–1154 – Hours: Appointment – Their vineyards sit at the top of Spring Mountain among other small wineries. Navigation Tip: They are located on the top of Spring Mountain. Take the road up the hill until you are on the top. After you pass the Schweiger winery on the right, look for a road going to the right and many mailboxes. There will also be winery signs. Turn right there and follow the signs for the number, 4060 and the winery name. This is the same drive that goes to the Barnett Winery. Map H

Signorello Vineyards – Hillside Perch – Wines: Cabernet Sauvignon, Zinfandel, Pinot Noir, Syrah, Sauvignon Semillon Blend 4500 Silverado Trail Napa CA 94558 – www.signorellovineyards.com – (707) 255–5990 – Hours: 10:30am–5:00am Appointment – A charming family winery on the hillsides of Silverado of Darioush. In 2024 they built a new winery. Map E3

Silver Oak Cellars – Big Popular Red Wines – Wines: Cabernet Sauvignon Blends – 915 Oakville Cross Road Oakville 94558 www.silveroak.com – (707) 944–8808 – Hours: 9am–5am – The winery building is constructed with antique blocks from an 1800's flour mill. The tasting room is spacious, the parking easy, and the buildings are easily seen from the Oakville Cross-road at the end of its long, tree–lined driveway. The wines are Cabernet blends from Napa Valley and Sonoma's Alexander Valley. They use American oak barrels, which gives the wine a stronger vanilla flavor. Map F3

Silverado Vineyards – Great Views in Stags Leap – Wines: Sauvignon Blanc, Chardonnay, Merlot, Sangiovese, Cabernet Sauvignon – 6121 Silverado Trail Napa 94558 – www.silveradovineyards.com – (707) 257–1770 – Hours: 10:30am–5pm – Silverado is romantic, with its California Mission style building, perched on a hill in the Stags Leap district, with gorgeous views over the vineyards from the patio, or from the comfortable tasting room. The wines are well made and properly priced. The staff is friendly and accustomed to visitors from all over the world. The drive up to the top of their hill seems steeper than it really is, but the convex mirrors allow you to see around the corners. Take your wine out on the patio and enjoy the view. There is something special about this place, with its collection of small, rounded hills that gathers the morning fog and holds it there as the Sun rises, sending rainbows through the vines. Map E3

Sinegal Estate – Wines: Bordeaux and Burgundy – 2125 Inglewood Ave Saint Helena, CA 94574 – www.sinegalestate.com – (707) 244–1187 – Hours: Appointment – The manor house and gardens go back many years, but the hospitality center is new that is designed encourage a social scene. It is tucked at the end of road at the foot of the Mayacamas mountains just south of Saint Helena. Map G2

Smith-Madrone – Spring Mountain Riesling – Wines: Cabernet Sauvignon, Chardonnay, Riesling – 4022 Spring Mountain Road Saint Helena CA 94574 – www.smithmadrone.com – (707) 963–2283 – Hours: Appointment – They did their first vintage in 1977. They are down home and relaxed. Map H

Sodaro Estate Winery and Vineyard – Coombsville – Wines: Cabernet Sauvignon, Cabernet Franc, Blends – 24 Blue Oak Lane Napa CA 94558 – www.sodarowines.com – (707) 975–6689 – Hours: Appointment for Purchases – This charming winery on the east side of Napa sits on a small hill and the tasting is on the patio over looking the valley. Map D

Somnium Wine – Downtown Calistoga Tasting Room – Wines: Cabernet Sauvignon – PO Box 307, Saint Helena CA 94574 – www.somniumwine.com – Deer Park CA 94508 – (707) –287–2246 – Hours: Appointment. The vineyards of Danica Patrick are on the steep, rocky hillsides of Howell Mountain. The 24–acre estate property includes six organic planted acres of Cabernet Sauvignon, Cabernet Franc, and Petit Verdot. As of 2021 the property and winery were still under development, although they were already making wine. Map L Does not appear on map

Spelletich Family – Corporate Park Winery – Wines: Bordeaux and Burgundy – 2545 Napa Valley Corporate Dr, Suite C Napa, CA 94558 – www.spellwine.com – (707) 775–7300 – Hours: Appointment. Map A1 Does not appear on map

Spottswoode Winery – Downtown Saint Helena – Wines: Cabernet Sauvignon, Sauvignon Blanc, Blends – 1902 Madrona Ave. St. Helena CA 94574 – www.spottswoode.com – (707) 963–0134 – Hours: Appointment – This winery is at the edge of suburban St. Helena. The owner and winemaking team are almost all women. Their permit allows them limited visitors so book 6–8 weeks in advance for an appointment. This property has a lot of history, including their ghost winery from the 1800's, and the estate house and gardens, which are beautifully planted and part of the tour. They do small production. Map G5

Spring Mountain Vineyards – Classic Spring Mountain – Wines: Syrah, Cabernet Sauvignon, Sauvignon Blanc – 2805 Spring Mountain Road St. Helena CA 94574 – www.springmtn.com – (707) 967–4188 – Hours: 10:00am – 5:00pm This is a grand estate that has their wineries and mansion at the foot of Spring Mountain, and their vineyards stretch up the hillsides above them. They are one of the biggest vineyards on Spring Mountain, being a combination of several large properties. The mansion dates to the 1800's and it the house was used in the television series Falcon Crest. They taste beside the vineyards, in the caves or the mansion. They recently changed hands. Map H

St Claire Brown – Downtown Napa – Wines: 850 Vallejo Street Napa, CA 94558 – www.stclairbrown.com – (707) 255–5591 – Hours: 12:00pm – 6:00pm – Check Website. Map A2 Zone 2

St. Helena Winery – Collectors – Wine: Bordeaux – 100 Pratt Avenue, Saint Helena, CA 94574 – www.sthelenawinery.com – (707) 967–9463 – Hours: 10:00am – 4:00pm Monday Saturday Appointment – This is an ultra-premium winery just off the Silverado Trail, but you are better off approaching it from Highway 29. It is a pretty Napa style ranch house. Map J

St. Supéry Vineyards – Understated Elegance – Wines: Sauvignon Blanc, Cabernet Sauvignon, Merlot, Chardonnay, Unoaked Chardonnay, Syrah, Cabernet Franc – 8440 St Helena Highway (Highway 29). Rutherford CA 94558 – www.stsupery.com – (707) 963–4507 – Hours: 10:00am – 5:00pm Appointment – They are owned by Chanel and fronted by a beautiful Victorian house, but the tasting room and winery is modern. Many of the grapes are sourced from Pope Valley. Find a place at the bar away from the entrance. Map F3

Staglin Family Vineyard – Premium – Wines: Chardonnay, Cabernet Sauvignon, Sangiovese – 1570 Bella Oaks Lane Rutherford CA 94573 www.staglinfamily.com – (707) 963–3994 Hours: 11:00am – 3:00pm Monday–Friday Appointment – This is a well–respected family–run winery with stellar wines that is known for their architecture, their organic methods and philanthropic work. They have a large cave. Map F3

Stag's Leap Wine Cellars – The Judgment of Paris Winner – Wines: Sauvignon Blanc, Chardonnay, Merlot, Cabernet Sauvignon – 5766 Silverado Trail Napa 94558 – www.cask23.com (707) 261–6441 – Hours: 10:00am – 4:30pm Appointment The Stags Leap district is in the southeastern corner of the Napa Valley. It is also the name of two wineries separated by an apostrophe. Stag's Leap Wine Cellars is one of Napa's most famous wineries for its win in the Judgment of Paris wine tasting in 1976 when their Cabernet Blend took the top position. The original family sold it in 2008 to Antinori and Chateau St Michele. They constructed a very modern hospitality center next to the caves with wonderful views of their vineyards and the hillsides beyond including the Stags Leap Peak. They do cave tours and seated tastings by appointment and their cave tasting room can accommodate a large group, in case you are planning a corporate event. The wines are authentic Stags Leap Region. Map F3

Stags' Leap Winery – Petite Syrah – Wines: Viognier, Chardonnay, Merlot, Cabernet Sauvignon, Petite Syrah – 6150 Silverado Trail Napa CA 94558 – www.stagsleapwinery.com – (707) 944–1303 – Hours: Appointment – This winery has tons of history and stories back to the 1800's. They taste in the Ivy–covered Manor House, which has been featured in both television and movies. Plan on making your plans well in advance. Because of the similarity of their name with their neighbors, Stag's Leap Wine Cellars, people often become confused and call the wrong winery. It was their neighbor that won the Judgment of Paris for their Cabernet. However, this winery's approach is much different, and they are most known for their less traditional wines, especially their fantastic Petite Syrah. It is currently owned by Beringer. Map F3

Sterling Vineyards – Ride the Gondola to Wine and Views – Wines: Cabernet Sauvignon, Merlot, Chardonnay, Pinot Noir, Shiraz, Sauvignon Blanc, Blends – 1111 Dunaweal Lane Calistoga 94515 – www. sterlingvineyards.com – (707) 942–3344 Hours: 10:00am – 4:30pm This iconic winery south of Calistoga is famous for the aerial tramway that brings you to the mountain top tasting room. It is a fun time, with great views and a wide variety of wines. Allow at least two hours for your visit. As you travel north and pass Larkmead Lane you can see Sterling's bright white building perched on its hilltop. Note: The 2020 Glass Fire scorched the hillsides around Sterling and they have removed numerous trees but they installed a new tramway and as of 2024 they up and running. Map K

Stony Hill Vineyard – Tucked Away – Wines: Chardonnay, Cabernet Franc – 3331 North St Helena Highway (Highway 29) Saint Helena CA 94574 – www.stonyhillvineyard.com – (707) 963–2636 – Hours: Appointment – This is a small winery up a long narrow road.
Saying that it is on Highway 29 is not accurate. You enter via the drive to the Bale Grist Mill and then just before the park's entrance you take the drive to the left which goes to the winery. The property started off as a family home that became vineyards and a winery. The tasting may be a bit of ride, but it is well worth the time. In 2023 the hospitality center was redone. Map J

Storybook Mountain Winery – The Northern Edge – Wines: Zinfandel, Cabernet Sauvignon – 3835 Highway 128 Calistoga CA 94515 – www.storybookwines.com – (707) 942–5310 –Hours: Monday–Saturday by Appointment – This is a beautiful location on the edge between the Napa Valley and Knight's Valley. The tour/tasting is normally done by the owners. It is a special place, although a bit of a ride. The tasting is done in the caverns dug into the hills in the 1800's. Map K

Strala Vineyards – Premium Wines Tasted at Brasswood – Wines: Bordeaux and Burgundy Blends – 5 Financial Plaza, Napa, CA 94559 (707) 339–2244 – Hours: Appointment – www.stralavineyards.com – A family with deep connections in the grape growing and wine making that produce good wines well priced for the quality. Map J

Sullivan Vineyards Winery – A Rambling Family Winery – Wines: Rosé, Chardonnay, Bordeaux Blend, Cabernet Sauvignon, Merlot – 1090 Galleron Road Saint Helena CA 94574 www.sullivanwine.com – (877) 244–7337 – Hours: 10:00am–5:00pm Appointment – They make big red wines and create a gracious tasting experience at their property behind the Prisoner Winery. The tasting room is elegant, and the outside patio is delightful with pond in the distance. Map G2

Summit Lake Vineyards and Winery – Howell Mountain – Wines: Cabernet Sauvignon, Zinfandel, Zinfandel Port – 2000 Summit Lake Dr. Angwin CA 94508 – www.summitlakevineyards.com – (707) 965–2488 – Hours: by Appointment - This is a small family winery about 20 minutes from the Silverado Trail. The tasting is at the home of the owners and the tasting is outside in the garden if weather permits. Their first commercial vintage was in 1978 and won gold medals. They do small production on site, and some wines are only available at the winery. For the quality, the prices are good. Map I

Sutter Home Winery – Big Selling Brand – Wines: Variety of modestly priced wines – 277 St Helena Highway South (Highway 29). Saint Helena 94574 – www.sutterhome.com – (707) 963–3104 – Hours: 10:00am–5:00pm – One of Napa's biggest wineries, but the grapes are from other areas. Known for White Zinfandel, one of the biggest selling wines in America. The Trinchero family, own numerous wineries in Napa. It is a big, spacious tasting room with a friendly staff, a wide variety of wines and a nice gift shop. The tastings are modest, as is the price point. Many of their Zinfandel grapes come from Amador County, in the Sierra Madre foothills. That was gold rush country and viticulture was started there by miners who saw that as a good alternative to panning for gold. Their Amador county, deep red Zinfandel is their stand–out wine and a good deal. White Zinfandel is miss–named, being a pink wine, the original wine was dry and white. It started off as a 'throw away juice', drawn off before fermentation so that the remainder would make a deeper, richer Zinfandel. One year they got sloppy and left some skins in the juice, and then the fermentation got stuck leaving some residual sugar. This pink, sweet accident was 'White Zinfandel'. They were stuck with the name and it has been a big seller ever since. Map G2

Swanson Vineyards – Transition – Wines: Merlot, Pinot Grigio, Rosato, Petite Syrah, Sangiovese, Syrah, Chardonnay, Blends, Muscat – www.swansonvineyards.com – Hours: Appointment The winery location was sold and the tastings are being done at Girard. Map K

Tamber Bey – Wine Making with Horses in Calistoga – Wines: Bordeaux, Burgundy – 1251 Tubbs Ln, Calistoga, CA 94515 – www.tamber-bey.com – (707) 942–2100 – Built into an active stable and paddocks that are home to various horses. They have a wonderful pairing that shows off their wines. It is a unique experience. These were once called the Sun Dance Stables which were owned in part by Robert Redford, who had a home just down the Silverado Trail for many years. It was a covered riding rink because he preferred riding in the shade. Map K

Taylor Family Vineyards – Stags Leap – Wines: Bordeaux – P.O. Box 2576, Napa CA 94558 – www.taylorfamilyvineyards.com – (707) 255–3593 – Hours: 10:00am – 5:00pm Monday Friday by Appointment – A lovely property sits in the heart of the famous Stags Leap District. The family personally planted the steep hillside vineyards. They typically pour on their patio that overlooks the valley. The wines are seriously good. They are located just south of the Silverado Vineyards, there is no sign, look for the number. Map E3

Taplin Cellars – Collectors – St Helena – Wines: Bordeaux and Burgundy – 1677 Lewelling Ln, St Helena, CA 94574 – www.taplincellars.com – (707) 968–9418 – Hours: Appointment – The Taplin family's history in Napa goes back to the 1800's. The vineyards are on the valley floor at the foot of the Mayacamas Mountains. It is family run and completely authentic. Map G2

Teachworth – Collectors – Wines: Bordeaux – 4451 Saint Helena Highway, Calistoga CA 94515 – www.teachworthcabs.com (707) 942–8432 – Hours: 10:00am – 4:00pm Appointment – Guest House Available for members – In the hills south of downtown Calistoga. Does not appear on map

Tedeschi – Calistoga Relaxed – Wines: Bordeaux, Burgundy 2779 Grant Street, Calistoga CA 94515 – www.tedeschifamilywinery.com – (707) 501–0668 – Hours: 10:00am – 5:00pm Appointment This little family winery produces a wonderful array of good quality wines at reasonable prices inside the Calistoga city limits. It is run by the multi-generation family and it is surrounded by their vineyards. Map K

The Crane Assembly – Collectors Old Vines – Wines: Bordeaux and Burgundy – PO Box 989, Saint Helena CA 94574 – www.thecraneassembly.com – (707) 302–0989 – Hours: Appt. Not on map

The Terraces – Adventurous – Wines: Zinfandel, Cabernet Sauvignon, Balsamic vinegar – 1450 Silverado Trail, Rutherford CA 94574 – www.terraceswine.com – (707) 963–1707 – Hours: 10:00am – 4:30pm Thursday–Sunday Appointment – Purchase is Required - They do their tour of this beautiful property in a 4–wheel drive. They have some of the few Zinfandel vines left in that section of Napa. They also make Balsamic vinegar. Map f4

The Wine Foundry – South Napa Industrial Park – Wines: – 45 Enterprise Ct STE 3, Napa Ca 94558 – www.thewinefoundry.com – Hours: 8:30am – 5:30pm Monday–Friday –Appointment – A custom crush facility that hosts various wineries. Map A1 Does not appear on map

Theorem Vineyards – Premium Calistoga – Wines: Bordeaux and Burgundy Blends – 255 Petrified Forest Road, Calistoga CA 94515 – www.theoremvineyards.com – (707) 942–4254 - On the site of the Graeser Winery. It was purchased a wealthy couple who transformed into a luxury winery. Map K

Titus – Silverado Trail – Wines: Bordeaux and Burgundy – 2971 Silverado Trail, Saint Helena CA 94574 – www.titusvineyards.com – (707) 963–3235 – This winery sits on the west side of the Silverado Trail north of downtown Saint Helena, surrounded by their vineyards. They are long time growers who produce a solid wine and pour it on their lovely patio in site of the vines. Map J

Tofanelli Family Vineyards – Calistoga Family Established 1929 – Wines: Charbono, Grenache, Petite Syrah, Zinfandel – 1212 Pine Street, Calistoga CA 94515 – www.tofanelliwine.com (707) 942–6504 – 10:00am to 4:30pm Appointment – They produce small lots of traditional grape varietals that were once widely planted in Napa Valley. The wine is made by the family and reasonably priced. Map K

Tom Eddy Winery – Calistoga Tiny – Wines: Bordeaux & Burgundy – 3870 CA–128, Calistoga, CA 94515 – www.tomeddywinery.com – (707) 942–4267 – Hours: 10:00am – 4:00pm Appointment – This family winery is far up the valley. The office tasting room is simple, but the walk to the caves is part of what makes this special, as well as the excellent wines. Map K

Tom Scott – Collectors – Wine: Cabernet Sauvignon – 1465 Yountville Cross Rd, Yountville, CA 94599 – www.tomscottvineyard.com – (707) 944–1850 – Hours: Appointment – This is a small family vineyard that makes one Cabernet blend. Map E3

Trefethen Vineyards – Historic Winery – Wines: Dry Riesling, Viognier, Chardonnay, Pinot Noir, Cabernet Franc, Merlot, Cabernet Sauvignon, Late Harvest Riesling – 1160 Oak Knoll Ave. Napa CA 94558 – www.trefethen.com – (707) 255–7700 Hours: 10:00am – 4:30pm Appointment – They are in an historic restored, gravity fed winery from the 1800's. The first floor is the barrel room that you see through a glass wall. The tasting room upstairs is spacious, and they make estate wines of high quality, inlcuding an outstanding Riesling, rare in Napa. Navigation Tip: As you come north on Highway 29, you turn right at the light at Oak Knoll Ave. The entrance is on the left. Map E2

Tres Perlas – Los Carneros Small Family for Collectors – Wines: Bordeaux and Burgundy Blends – 625 Imperial Way #6, Napa, CA 94559 – www.tresperlas.com – (707) 255-0786. Map C Does not appear on map

Tres Sabores – Small Rustic Charm – Wines: Zinfandel, Cabernet Sauvignon, Petite Syrah, Petite Verdot, Sauvignon Blanc 1620 South Whitehall Lane Saint Helena CA 94574 – www.tressabores.com – (707) 967–8027 – Hours: by Appointment This is a charming family winery on prime bench land with old Zin and Cab vines. In nice weather, the tasting is done outside at a picnic table, under huge olive trees. In cool weather, the tasting is done in the winery. The hillsides are planted with grapes and pomegranates. Watch for the sheep in the vineyards as you arrive because this is a working ranch. This is hands–on winemaking so if you can, visit here during crush. Map G2

Trinchero Napa Valley – Saint Helena Wine and Food – Wines: Cabernet Sauvignon, Meritage, Sauvignon Blanc, Merlot, Petite Verdot – 3070 St Helena Highway (Highway 29). Saint Helena CA 94574 – www.trincherowinery.com – (707) 963–3104 – This hospitality center just north of Saint Helena, showcases their best wines & culinary center. Map J

Trinitas Cellars – At the Meritage Resort – Wines: Chardonnay, Pinot Noir, Mataro, Petit Syrah, Zinfandel, Blends – 875 Bordeaux Way Napa CA 94558 www.trinitascellars.com – (707) 251 –1956 – Hours: 12:00pm – 8:00pm. Their tasting room is in a cave behind the hotel that they share with the spa. So many of the people who stay at the resort visit them. They produce less common varietals and they are worth the visit just for that, although the entire experience is cool. Map A1

Truchard Vineyard – Carneros Gem – Wines: Chardonnay, Roussanne, Pinot Noir, Syrah, Zinfandel, Merlot, Cabernet Franc, Cabernet Sauvignon, Petit Verdot, Tempranillo, Olive Oil – 3234 Old Sonoma Road Napa CA 94559 – www.truchardvineyards.com – (707) 253–7153 – Hours: Appointment – The Truchard family makes wonderful wines, complex, delicious and interesting, at their property in the hills of Los Carneros. They have owned the land since 1974 and started making their own wines in 1989. They make a Cabernet Sauvignon, which is rare in Carneros, an area generally too cool for this heat loving grape. The tasting room is basic, the caves are nice, and in good weather they taste outside on the lawn beside the house.   Map C

Tulocay Winery – Eastern Napa – Wines: Pinot Noir, Cabernet Sauvignon, Merlot, Syrah, Zinfandel, Chardonnay – 1426 Coombsville Rd Napa CA 94558 – www.tulocaywinery.com – (707) 255–4064 – Hours: Appointment – This is old school Napa, totally authentic and close to the downtown. Map D

Turnbull Wine Cellars – Photo Gallery in the Middle of Oakville Wines: Sauvignon Blanc, Old Bull Red, Viognier, Toroso, Cabernet Sauvignon, Merlot, Barbera, Syrah – 8210 St Helena Highway (Highway 29). Oakville CA 94562 – www.turnbullwines.com – (707) 963–5839 – Hours: 10:00am to 4:30pm – The original owner, William Turnbull, was the architect who designed numerous wineries including the Cakebread winery next door, so note the similarity. It features a photography gallery'. They have a nice tasting room and grounds. Map F3

Twenty Rows / Vinoce – Tannery Row Commercial Space Tasting Room – Wines: Bordeaux and Burgundy Blends – 68 South Coombs Street, L6 Napa, CA 94559 – www.twentyrows.com – (707)–265–7750 – Hours: 11:00am to 6:00pm Wednesday – Saturday, 12:00pm to 6:00pm Sunday Appointment. Map A2 Does not appear on map

Twomey Cellars – **CLOSED** 2025 - Merlot Focus – Wines: Merlot, Pinot Noir, Sauvignon Blanc – 1183 Dunaweal Lane Calistoga CA 94515 – www.twomeycellars.com – (707) 942–2489 – Hours: 9:00am – 4:00pm This winery is associated with Silver Oak. They created this winery to specialize in Merlot based wines. The Twomey winery in northern Sonoma specializes in Pinot Noir. Map K

Varozza Vineyards – Saint Helena Dry Farmed Five Generations – Wines: Bordeaux and Burgundy – 514 Pratt Ave, St Helena, CA 94574 – www.varozzavineyards.com – (707) 963–0331 – A family estate winery north of downtown Saint Helena. They are traditional Italian American growers who started here in the late 1800's. Dry farming produces less grapes that are known for their rich flavors. The wines are moderately priced. Map J

Velo Vino (Clif Family) – Downtown Saint Helena Tasting Room and Retail Shop – Wines: Cabernet Sauvignon – 709 Main St, St Helena, CA 94574 –www.cliffamily.com – (707) 968–0625 – Hours: 10:00am to 5:00pm – Bike Rental Packages, Breakfast Pairings and Cheese and Jam Boards – This is the family that makes the Clif Bar, which you will find for sale there. Map G5

Venge Vineyards – Wines: Bordeaux and Burgundy –4708 Silverado Trail N, Calistoga, CA 94515 – www.vengevineyards.com (707) 942–9100 – Hours: 10:00am – 4:30pm Appointment – The Venges, father and son, are well known consulting winemakers. This is the son's winery in a modern metal building in the northern the valley. Fortunately, the tastings take place in a cozy house next door. Map K

Vermeil Wines – Downtown Napa Tasting Room – Wines: Sauvignon Blanc, Charbono, Cabernet Franc, Cabernet Sauvignon, Zinfandel – 1018 First Street, Napa, CA 94559 – www.vermeilwines.com – (707) 254–9881 – Hours: 11:00am – 11:00pm Appointment – Owned by former football coach Dick Vermeil. Map A2 Zone 2

VGS Potelle – Saint Helena Tasting Room – Wines: Bordeaux and Burgundy – 1200 Dowdell Lane, Saint Helena CA 94574 www.vgschateaupotelle.com – (707) 255–9440 – Hours: 10:00am – 5:00pm Appointment – Marvelous wines with a French style by a French wine maker who has making wine here for many years. The initials stand for 'Very Good Shit!' Map G5

Viader – Deer Park Cab Franc – Wines: Bordeaux, Syrah, Tempranillo – 1120 Deer Park Road Deer Park CA 94574 – www.viader.com – (707) 963–3816 – Hours: 10:00am–4:30pm Appointment – This family–run winery makes Cabernet Franc blends. Great views! The gate is on the left at a sharp, climbing curve so be careful of the cars coming down the hill. Their neighboring winery was destroyed in the 2020 Glass fire. Map I

Vice Versa Winery – Collectors – Saint Helena Town Tasting Room – Wines: Bordeaux Blends – 707–968–5620 – Hours: Appointment www.viceversawine.com – They have vineyards in Calistoga and produce marvelous wines. Map G5 Does not appear on map

Villa Ragazzi – Very Small Oakville Winery – Wines: Sangiovese – 7878 Money Rd, Napa, CA 94558 – www.villaragazziwine.com – (707) 486–3184 – Hours: Appointment – The name means 'house of the kids', this is a tiny family estate vineyard owned by the winemakers, where they make just over a hundred cases of wine yearly.   Map F3 Does not appear on map

Vin Roc Wine Caves – Collectors in Southeast Napa Valley Wines: Bordeaux – 4069 Atlas Peak Rd, Napa, CA 94558 – www.vinrocnapa.com – (707) 265–0943 – Appt. Does not appear on map

Vincent Arroyo Winery – Calistoga – Wines: Cabernet Sauvignon, Merlot, Petite Syrah, Chardonnay, Sangiovese, Port, Blends 2361 Greenwood Ave. Calistoga CA 94515 – www.vincentarroyo.com (707) 942–6995 – Hours: 10:00am – 4:00pm Appointment – They are located just north of downtown Calistoga south of Chateau Montelena. The overall feeling is that of a small working winery without any pretensions. They are in the second generation now. Map K

Vine Cliff Winery – CLOSED – Wines: Cabernet Sauvignon, Chardonnay, Merlot. – 7400 Silverado Trail Yountville CA 94599 – www.vinecliff.com – Map E3

Vine Hill Ranch – Collectors Oakville – Wines: Cabernet Sauvignon – www.vinehillranch.com – 707–944–8130 – The family has owned these vineyards since the 1950's, and they supply grapes to many local wineries. Map E2 Does not appear on map

Vineyard 29 – Look for the Sign because they are located at 2929 Highway 29 – Wines: Cabernet Sauvignon, Cabernet Franc,

Sauvignon Blanc, Zinfandel, Blends – 2929 Highway 29 North Saint Helena CA 94574 – www.vineyard29.com – (707) 963–9292 – Hours: Tuesday–Saturday Appointment – This state of the art winery north of downtown Saint Helena is on a hillside with great views of the valley. Plan for a tour of the caves where the tasting takes place. Map J

Vineyard 7 and 8 – Collectors – Spring Mountain Collectors Wines: Bordeaux – Spring Mountain Road, Saint Helena CA 94574 – www.vineyard7and8.com – (707) 963–9425 – Hours: Appointment, closed weekends – This winery at the top of Spring Mountain is for the enthusiast. From the front it looks like a house, but from the back it is obviously a serious winery with great views. The name comes from the Asian numerological significance of those two numbers. Map H

Vineyardist – Collectors – www.thevineyardist.com – (707) 942–0120 – Hours: 10:00am – 2:00pm Appt – The original vineyards were planted in the 1880's by a Danish ship captain off Petrified Forest Road in Calistoga. Map K

Vintner's Collective Tasting Room – Numerous premium labels in downtown Napa – 1245 Main Street Napa CA 94559 – www.vintnerscollective.com – (707) 255–7150 – Hours: 11:00am to 6:00pm. One of Napa's oldest collective tasting rooms. Map A2 Zone 2

V. Madrone – Small – Wines: Chardonnay, Cabernet Sauvignon, Petite Syrah, Zinfandel. – 3199 Saint Helena Highway North Saint Helena CA 94574 – www.vmadrone.com – (877) 994–6311 – Hours: Appointment – This is a small, charming premium winery, although the vineyards are nearby, just north of downtown St. Helena. AXR winery is located on the same property. Map J

Volker Eisele – Collectors – Wines: Bordeaux, Burgundy – Lower Chiles Valley Road, Saint Helena CA 94574 – www.volkereiselefamilyestate.com – (707) 965–9485 – A small, premium winery in the hills of eastern Napa. Their redwood winery barn was constructed in the 1800's. *Note: 2020 Glass fire came through there. Map F5*

V. Sattui Winery – The Famous Deli and Winery – Wines: The valley's widest selection – 1111 White Lane Saint Helena 94574 (On Highway 29) – www.vsattui.com – (707) 963–7774 – Hours: 9:00am – 6:00pm, 9:00am – 5:00pm in Winter – This may be Napa's busiest winery thanks to its large deli and picnic tables. Centrally located, the wines are also middle of the road, and very drinkable with a reserve tasting room by appointment. The property is pretty, although it suffers from the crowds. The founder owns Castello di Amorosa in Calistoga. They are in a commercial zone, and not in the Agricultural Preserve. The other property with that 'deli' exemption is Brasswood. Map G2

Wheeler Farms – Saint Helena Collectors – Wines: Bordeaux and Burgundy – 588 Zinfandel Lane, Saint Helena CA 94574 www.wheelerfarmswine.com – (707) 200–8500 – Hours: 10:00am – 4:00pm Appointment – This newer winery from a long-time wine making family is a biodynamic gem. It is very convenient south of St. Helana and the property is extensively planted with food plants. The Winery is state of the art. Map G2

Whetstone – Tasting Site in an Historic Building with Burgundy Style wines – Wines: Pinot Noir, Chardonnay – 1075 Atlas Peak Road, Napa CA 94558 – www.whetstonewinecellars.com - (707) 254–0600 Hours: 10:30am – 3:30pm Appointment – Tastings generally take place outside in their garden in front of the old distillery building from the late 1800's. It is in the south eastern corner of the valley just north of Monticello Road, which is the eastern extension of Trancas Avenue, which is the northern edge of the City of Napa. The vineyards and winery are at a different location. Mapa E3

Whitehall Lane Winery – Fun with Wonderful Wines – Wines: Cabernet Sauvignon, Merlot, Chardonnay, Belmuscato Dessert Wine – 1563 St Helena Highway (Highway 29). South Saint Helena CA 94574 – www.whitehalllane.com – (707) 963–7035 Hours: 11:00am – 5:45pm – The modern tasting room has a bit of a bar feel, but it allows diverse groups to mix. Map F3

White Rock Vineyards – Soda Canyon – Wines: Bordeaux and Burgundy – 1112 Loma Vista Dr Napa, CA 94558 – www.whiterockvineyards.com – (707) 257–7922 – Hours: 10:00am – 5:00pm Appointment – A small family winery in the hills in southeastern Napa off Soda Canyon Road. Map E3

William Cole – Saint Helena Collectors – Cabernet Blends – 2849 St Helena Hwy, St Helena, CA 94574 – www.williamcolevineyards.com – (707) 963-6100 – These fifth generation Napa winemakers produce less than a thousand cases of wine from three small vineyards around the county. The building was constructed in 1873 and the upper part is a home, while the ground floor is the winery. William and Cole are the first names of the father and son team who make the wine. They have a beautifully appointed tasting room. The winery is wonderfully convenient, located on the west side of Highway 29 north of Saint Helena, by the intersection of Deer Park Road. They share the driveway with the stone Morlet Winery, built in 1880, which is more visible from the road. Map G5

William Harrison Vineyards – A Great Story – Wines: Cabernet Sauvignon, Cabernet Franc, Chardonnay – 1443 Silverado Trail Saint Helena CA 94574 – www.whwines.com – (707) 963–8310 – Hours: 11–5 Thursday – Monday – This is a rustic and slightly eccentric tasting room for a family with a great story that goes back to the 1500's in Italy. The wines are interesting, and the location is great. Watch out for the stuffed bear that comes with a story! They have a nice patio for tastings and it is surrounded by their Cabernet Franc vineyards. Map F4

William Hill Estate – Not Accepting Visitors - Southern Valley – Wines: Chardonnay, Merlot, Cabernet Sauvignon, Cabernet Franc, Malbec, Petit Verdot, Estate Meritage – 1761 Atlas Peak Road Napa CA 94558 www.williamhillestate.com – (707) 265–3024 – Hours: 10:00am–5:00pm Appointment. This is a great site, with a picnic area under an arbor. It is owned by Gallo. Map E3

The Wine Thief – Downtown Tasting Room at the Oxbow – Wines: Cabernet Sauvignon, Burgundy – 708 1st St, Napa, CA 94559 (707) 666–2650 – Hours: 10:00am – 6:00pm Appt.Map A2 Zone 4

Yates Family Vineyard – Mt Veeder – Wines: Cabernet Sauvignon, Cabernet Franc, Merlot – 3104 Redwood Rd Napa – www.YatesFamilyVineyard.com – (707) 226–1800 – Hours: Appointment – A small family winery in southwestern Napa, on the way to Mount Veeder. Map B

Y. Rousseau – Corporate Park – Wines: Bordeaux, General French – 902 Enterprise Way Suite O Napa, CA 94558 – www.yrousseau-wines.com – (707) 332–4524 – Hours: 9:00am – 4:00pm Monday–Saturday Appointment. Map A1 Does not appear on map

Young Inglewood – Collectors – Wines: Bordeaux and Burgundy – 1919 Inglewood Ave, Saint Helena CA 94574 – www.younginglewood.com – (707) 200–4572 – A premium winery selling through allocation. Map G2

Zakin Family Estate – By Allocation – Wines: Cabernet Sauvignon – 290 Crystal Springs Rd Saint Helena CA 94574 – www.zakinwines.com – (415)–793–6354 – An ultra-premium family winery using the winemaker Phillipe Melka. Map G3

ZD Wines – Silverado Savvy – Wines: Chardonnay, Pinot Noir, Cabernet Sauvignon – 8383 Silverado Trail Napa CA 94558 www.zdwines.com – (800) 487–7757 – Hours: 10:00am –4:30pm Appointment – They have a friendly, relaxed, stylish tasting room, with a patio on the second story that overlooks their organic vineyards, a nice staff, and some good wine. They often get missed because they are below the road on a downhill section of the Silverado Trail, so you do not see them until you are at the driveway. They are to the south of Mumm Napa on the Silverado Trail. the name comes from the term 'Zero Defects', because the founders came from the aeronautic industry. The wine maker is from their third generation. This is a winery worth visiting, organic, with a great family history. As you leave notice the sign 'Organic since 1999'. Map G3

Other Titles by These Authors

AmicisTours.com

A Tour Guide's Napa Valley
A Tour Guide's Sonoma Wine Country
Sonoma Navigator, Maps & Highlights
Napa Navigator, Maps & Highlights
Wine Country in Shorts, A Tour Guide's Stories

Catch Our TV Show & Podcast 'Wine in Shorts'

PlanetaryCalendar.com
Published Annually since 1949

Planetary Calendar Astrology Forecasts & Health Hints
Two Wall Sizes, a Pocket Size, a Day Planner &
a Digital Version for your Phone and Computer
The Lunar Wine Tasting Calendar
The Companion Book
'Planetary Calendar Astrology,
Moving Beyond Observation to Action'
Reclaiming Astrology from the Partriarchy
*Watch the Author's Monthly Forecasts
at Planetary Calendar.com*

SpaceAndTime.com

From the 'Tango' Series
Feng Shui and the Tango, The Dance of Design
Feng Shui and the Tango, The Essential Chapters
25th Anniversary Edition
FS&T Prosperity Lessons
FS&T Happiness Lessons
The Dream Desk Quiz
Creating Clarity

About the Authors, the Books, & Amicis Winery Tours

Ralph and Lahni DeAmicis found their way into writing tour and travel books by starting to create a book about winery buildings for their series on Feng Shui, but the research was going excruciatingly slow. While the winery staff knew the wines, they rarely knew about the buildings. Then one day, while coming out of the Stag's Leap Wine Cellars, Ralph chatted up a local limousine driver who was a wealth of information about interesting winery buildings, apparently that knowledge was part of a tour guide's toolbox.

Seeing a research opportunity that would also put some money in their pockets, Ralph got a part time job driving tours, coming home daily with notes and photographs of the wineries. As he navigated his way around the various valleys, they realized that even though the wineries are the biggest attraction, there wasn't a good 'winery' tour book. So, their project about winery buildings morphed into their first guidebook in 2008, becoming the first in a series of updates and improvements.

After two years of touring for other companies Ralph & Lahni decided to start their own tour company, Amicis Tours, to make the continuing research easier. They soon realized that it's a fun business that brings them to beautiful places while connecting them to the winemaking community and visitors from around the world, they are both multi-lingual. In 2012 they started producing the TV show 'Wine Country at Work' which allowed them to more deeply explore topics that they found interesting.

In 2023 they added a new book, The 2023 Wine Tasting Calendar, that uses the position of the Moon to provide guidance about to manage a wine tasting. The 2024 edition is out and 2025 is underway. Enjoy, and travel safely and happily!

Find their books and videos at:
www.AmicisTours.com
Cuore Libre Publishing
Books and Calendars

Other Titles by These Authors

From the Back Cover of
2025 Lunar Wine Tasting Calendar
From Wine Tasting with the Stars
by Ralph & Lahni DeAmicis

For centuries humanity has linked wine to the celestial. Galileo wrote, "Wine is sunshine held together by water." Dom Pérignon, called out when he discovered champagne, "Come quickly, I'm tasting stars!" Collectors revere the famous 'Comet Vintages' for their amazing longevity.

Biodynamic winemakers use astrological calendars for timing vineyard and cellar tasks and tasting room events. 'Tasting with the Stars' brings together the worlds of wine and astrology in ways that illuminate them both.

Combining chapters from four books, the authors offer their nique insights as wine tour guides and astrologers, explaining the fascinating parallels between the planets and popular grape varietals. It explains how knowing the Moon Sign will help you host the best possible wine tastings.

The astrology calendar is written in plain language to make this system easy to use, no matter your astrological knowledge. Additional chapters explore the Twelve Signs, and the ABC's of fine wine tasting. This is an introduction to the astrology of wine that will enhance your enjoyment for years to come.

Go to AmicisTours.com
to Find This and Our Other Titles

From the Back Cover of

Wine Country in Shorts
The Stories of Napa and Sonoma
by Ralph & Lahni DeAmicis

Sonoma and Napa were the northern most points in the Spanish Empire's expansion in the Americas. They clearly came to these beautiful valleys and thought, "We've arrived in Eden, we don't need to go any farther." This place was once considered the far ends of the Earth where explorers, adventurers and the foolish went, which attracted a very interesting demographic.

Sonoma and Napa, separated by the Mayacamas Mountains are quite different. Sonoma is like the older sister, a good-looking girl, a great cook and gardener, content with her family and friends. While Napa is her golden-haired little brother, endlessly curious about the outside world. Whenever he walks in the room, everybody makes a fuss, which drives Sonoma crazy, but Napa adores his big sister.

These stories and insights present a wonderfully revealing picture of this remarkable place. They were collected over twenty years by *Ralph and Lahni DeAmicis*, popular storytellers, speakers, team building leaders and filmmakers, who publish the region's most popular wine tour books.

Go to AmicisTours.com
to Find This and Our Other Titles